INTERNATIONAL RELATIONS

UNDERSTANDING THE BEHAVIOR OF NATIONS

CLOSE UP® FOUNDATION

Close Up Publishing

Director
George W. Dieter

Managing Editor
Amy E. Tarasovic

Senior Editor
Charles R. Sass

Writer
Susan Ballinger

Manager of Art, Production, and Scheduling
Tisha L. Finniff

Graphic Designer
Jennifer S. Gerstein

Supervisor of Editorial Support and Scheduling
Lucy Keshishian

Copyeditor and Proofreader
Margaret White

Photo Researcher
Matt Payne

Cover Photo
Renée Bouchard/
Close Up Foundation

© 2001 Close Up Foundation
Printed in the United States of America.

All rights reserved. No part of this book may be reproduced or used in any form or by any means, electronic or mechanical, including photocopying, recording, or by any information storage and retrieval system, without written permission of the publisher.

Close Up Foundation
Stephen A. Janger
President and Chief Executive Officer

The Close Up Foundation, a nonprofit, nonpartisan, civic education organization, informs, inspires, and empowers people to exercise the rights and accept the responsibilities of citizens in a democracy. Close Up connects individuals of all ages to their communities and institutions through challenging educational programs and products. By building partnerships with the education community, the private and philanthropic sectors, and all branches and levels of government, Close Up makes civic participation a dynamic and meaningful experience.

Close Up Publishing, a branch of the Close Up Foundation, produces books, teachers' guides, video documentaries, and other materials that develop critical thinking skills and stimulate interest in current issues, government, international relations, history, and economics. To find out more about Close Up's original and timely resources, call 800-765-3131 or visit www.closeup.org/pubs.htm.

Close Up Foundation
44 Canal Center Plaza
Alexandria, VA 22314-1592
www.closeup.org

CONTENTS

INTERNATIONAL RELATIONS TODAY 5

CHAPTER ONE
THE BEHAVIOR OF NATIONS 7
1.1 Defining National Interest 8
1.2 Developing Foreign Policy 11
1.3 The Tools of Foreign Policy 17

CHAPTER TWO
HOW U.S. FOREIGN POLICY IS MADE 25
2.1 The United States and the World 26
2.2 "An Invitation to Struggle": The President and Congress 27
2.3 Other Influences on Foreign Policy . . . 33

CHAPTER THREE
THE COLD WAR AND BEYOND 39
3.1 The Origins of the Cold War 40
3.2 Superpower Competition 45
3.3 "The End of History" 49
3.4 A New International System 52

CHAPTER FOUR
WORLD ISSUES TODAY 61
4.1 International Trade 62
4.2 Military Buildups 67
4.3 Nationalism and Ethnic Conflict 71
4.4 The Developing World 77
4.5 The Environment 83
4.6 The Twenty-First Century 87

APPENDICES
FOR FURTHER READING 89
WEB RESOURCES 92
GLOSSARY 93

INTERNATIONAL RELATIONS TODAY

During the Cold War, *international relations*—how countries relate to one another, how they work together, and how they conflict—were defined by the tense relationship between the United States and the Soviet Union. The Cold War came with its own set of clear rules that divided much of the world into two ideological camps: communism and capitalism. Many countries' alliances, conflicts, obligations, and priorities were automatically dictated by their choice of government during this time.

Since communism collapsed in the late 1980s and early 1990s, the dynamics of international relations have gone through fundamental changes. Alliances and priorities have shifted. Many countries are adopting free-market economies and more democratic styles of government. Unregulated by former Cold War barriers, nations are trading more freely with one another. Inexpensive communication technologies—including the Internet—have created more opportunities for people and countries to share ideas and trade products and services. This trend toward more open and free worldwide interaction has come to be known as *globalization,* and many people believe that it marks the beginning of an era defined by increased cooperation among nations, greater economic opportunities, and a higher standard of living for people in developing countries.

However, while the end of the Cold War and the onset of globalization have produced a number of beneficial results, the changes have come with their own set of problems. Without the strict control that Soviet-era dictators provided, many longstanding ethnic feuds within formerly communist countries have come to a boil. As nations have increased trade, they have also begun to compete more. Therefore, countries with weak economies and low technological capabilities fall further and further behind, and the gap between rich and poor grows. Moreover, the introduction of free markets in countries without a democratic tradition has created a number of problems, including increased corruption and crime, environmental degradation, and overpopulation of urban centers.

At the beginning of the twenty-first century, few nations have the luxury of acting in isolation. Decisions made by one nation—increasing a defense budget, regulating an industry, decreasing a federal deficit—can have a dramatic effect on other nations. Although the interdependence of the world encourages cooperation over conflict, it also makes international relations more complex and unpredictable. This interdependence is the modern challenge to countries when making foreign policy: to take advantage of the benefits of globalization while tackling the problems that it creates.

CHAPTER ONE

THE BEHAVIOR OF NATIONS

Today, events in one nation can affect many other nations and sometimes the entire world. An economic crisis in Asia spreads to Latin America and raises concern on Wall Street. Emissions from U.S.-owned factories operating in Mexico contribute to pollution in Texas. A refugee crisis in eastern Europe mobilizes relief efforts from around the world.

Once a collection of isolated nations, today's world is increasingly interdependent; some call it a global community. Governments share similar economic and security concerns, and modern methods of communication and transportation give world leaders access to information—and to one another—more quickly. Because the world is so closely linked, understanding the behavior of individual nations is critical to understanding world events.

1.1 DEFINING NATIONAL INTEREST

Most people act out of self-interest. They base their actions on what will be to their benefit or advantage. However, not all people define self-interest in the same way. For example, some value financial success more than anything else, so their actions reflect their desire to increase their personal wealth. Others value religious ideals and act according to their faith. Still others value power and seek ways to increase their authority over others.

Underlying the behavior of nations is the concept of *national interest*. Just as most people behave according to their own perception of what is best for them, on the national level, citizens look to their leaders to carry out policies that promote their nation's self-interest. At first glance, the idea of national interest may seem fairly simple: It is what is best for a particular nation. However, not all residents of a nation agree on what is best. Perceptions of national interest vary from person to person and evolve over time.

National interest is a combination of the security, economic, and ideological concerns of a country. Even though every nation in the world tries to meet certain basic needs so it can survive and improve its citizens' living standards, each nation is unique and has its own set of concerns. Some countries, such as Mali or Bangladesh, are concerned primarily with survival—with feeding their people or protecting themselves from attack. Others, like Niger or Malaysia, seek to develop their natural resources, so they can trade them for food and other commodities. Nations such as Japan and the United States have relatively little difficulty feeding their people and are more concerned with the continued growth of their industrial economies. Although every country in the world has a unique perception of its own national interest, all share three broad concerns: security, economics, and ideology.

SECURITY INTERESTS

The most basic interest of any nation, from the tiny island state of Grenada to the giant People's Republic of China, is ensuring its physical survival. National governments form armies to protect themselves from attack and join military alliances to bolster protection against more powerful foes.

Nations maintain armed forces to defend their security interests.

A nation's concern about security stems from its perception of outside threats. For example, Israel maintains a large, well-equipped military because it is surrounded by hostile neighbors. In contrast, Switzerland has a relatively small army because of its neutrality during the Cold War, its friendly relations with all European nations, and its protection provided by the mountainous regions near its borders.

But security interests mean more than just protection against outside attack. A nation must also ensure that social order is maintained and that its citizens are safe from violence and crime. To do this, countries must have laws to protect their people and a police force and legal system capable of enforcing those laws.

ECONOMIC INTERESTS

Countries seek to promote the economic welfare of their people. Economic interests of nations vary according to the availability of resources and the development of those resources.

Developing countries, like many in sub-Saharan Africa, need to obtain the basic necessities of life—food and water, shelter, and health care—for their people. They lack the agricultural methods or the manufacturing industries that would enable them to move beyond basic survival. Because they are unable to produce enough food, they trade raw materials or cash crops for food and advanced technology. Some developing countries also concentrate on attracting foreign investment and tourism to strengthen their economies.

Other nations, such as Germany and Japan, are highly industrialized and turn out a variety of products, including processed food, industrial machinery, automobiles, computers, software, and clothing. *Industrialized nations* usually produce more than they need. They then export these products—mostly manufactured goods—to other nations in exchange for needed raw materials, other finished products, or money.

The economic growth of many nations depends on their ability to buy and sell products or services abroad. Their economic interests are determined by the wants and needs of their citizens, the types of products they have to sell, and how developed their economies are.

Economic interests are determined by a country's needs, resources, and level of development.

IDEOLOGICAL INTERESTS

Security and economic concerns alone do not explain why nations behave as they do. Ideology—a combination of the beliefs, values, culture, religion, and historical experiences of a nation's people—also plays a role. All countries are interested in protecting their way of life at home, and many try to promote it abroad as well.

For example, U.S. leaders encourage people around the world to hold free elections because they believe

Nations work to protect and promote ideological interests at home and abroad.

cal security of their nation depends on adherence to a particular religion. Such leaders encourage their citizens to do whatever is necessary—including going to war—to defend ideological beliefs. Some countries are also willing to forego greater economic benefits to maintain their ideological interests.

The responsibility for defining the national interest falls to a nation's political leaders. In each country of the world, a national government assesses threats to its security, the health of its economy, and the strength of its ideology to determine its national interest.

democracy is the best form of government. Iran, on the other hand, believes that governments—particularly in the Middle East and North Africa—should follow the religion of Shi'ite Islam. Iranian leaders encourage other nations to adopt forms of government based on Islamic values and beliefs.

These three concerns—security, economics, and ideology—do not exist independently. Often, an economic or ideological concern is also a security concern. For example, if people do not have enough to eat, the stability and therefore the security of their government may be threatened. Some leaders believe that the physi-

NATIONAL INTEREST CONCERNS

Although every nation has a unique perception of its own national interest, all nations share three broad concerns: security, economics, and ideology. To determine its national interest, a national government assesses threats to its security, the health of its economy, and the strength of its ideology.

National Interest

Security Interests
- Protecting natural borders
- Maintaining relations with allies
- Ensuring the safety of citizens from violence and crime

Economic Interests
- Providing citizens with an adequate standard of living
- Ensuring economic development and growth
- Establishing trade relations with other nations

Ideological Interests
- Supporting a way of life at home and promoting it abroad
- Protecting the cultural and religious heritage of a nation
- Promoting a system of government

1.2 DEVELOPING FOREIGN POLICY

In every nation, leaders develop a *foreign policy*—or a course of action—to pursue the national interests of their countries. The ability of a nation to carry out its foreign policy is based on many factors, including its military and economic strength. A nation's power in these areas is determined mainly by its technological capabilities and geopolitical factors (geography and demographics).

In developing foreign policy, leaders generally try to balance their nation's immediate needs with its long-term goals. For example, a president whose people are facing malnutrition and mass starvation may give higher priority to trading for food than for high-tech equipment. In addition, new circumstances, such as a changing economy, a natural disaster, or the militarization of a hostile neighbor, can force leaders to reevaluate the needs of their country.

Leaders of all nations must carefully balance economic, military, and strategic considerations when developing foreign policy because their decisions will have far-reaching effects both at home and abroad.

POWER AND THE PURSUIT OF NATIONAL INTEREST

Powerful nations are more likely to reach their policy goals than less powerful ones. In international relations, power refers to a nation's ability to influence others.

For centuries, world leaders, philosophers, and scholars have tried to define the nature of power. Some thinkers have concluded that nations act to prevent any one country from becoming too powerful. According to this theory, if one country grows too strong, others will shift alliances and change policies to prevent the stronger nation from using or abusing its power. Others believe that weaker countries ally themselves with powerful ones to gain more influence in the world and to receive protection from the stronger ally.

Some nations have power because they occupy a strategic location or because they control a valuable resource. Others are powerful because they develop strong, diversified economies or formidable militaries. And sometimes a nation is strong because its people are willing to sacrifice anything to achieve that nation's goals. However, the most powerful are nations like the United States, which has many of these characteristics.

No nation has absolute power. The amount of power a country has is relative to that of other countries and is based on a combination of factors. An economist might think that Japan is powerful because of its efficient and prosperous economy. A military expert, on the other hand, might disagree because Japan relies heavily on the United States for military support. Economic and military strength add to a nation's stability—its security—and most leaders recognize that ensuring stability is in their nation's interest. World leaders agree, however, that a nation must have either economic or military power to be a major player on the global stage.

ECONOMIC POWER

Most world leaders and experts believe that a strong, diverse economy—not necessarily a large military—is the key to power and influence in the world today. Because nations increasingly rely on international trade for their own economic growth, countries are becoming more competitive. Leaders are constantly looking for the best market for their country's goods and services. If a nation has nothing to offer other countries in the way of products or markets, its standing in the world will be insignificant. On the other hand, the country that offers something to sell and possesses the wealth to buy foreign goods and services will be sought out by others.

After World War II, the Western allies, including the United States, pressured Japan and West Germany to demilitarize. Therefore, during the Cold War, these two nations spent little money on national defense and concentrated on improving their economies. By the 1980s, they had emerged as two of the most powerful countries on Earth. Other Asian countries have larger militaries, but Japan's advanced economy places it in a position of power and influence in both Asia and the world. Similarly, many call Germany "the engine of Europe" because of its economic, not its military, might.

Economic strength not only determines global power and influence but also is often the key to a nation's survival. Most leaders believe that a prosperous economy that provides citizens with jobs and a decent standard of living is essential to a country's national security. High unemployment and widespread poverty can destabilize countries and governments.

The breakup of the Soviet Union is a classic example of the importance of economic power. During the Cold War, the size of the Soviet Union's military and

COUNTRY PROFILES

Total Land Area (sq mi)**
United States	3,536,341
Japan	145,874
Germany	137,838
Mexico	761,600
Iran	636,243
Nigeria	356,700

Population**
United States	275,562,673
Japan	126,549,976
Germany	82,797,408
Mexico	100,349,766
Iran	65,619,636
Nigeria	123,337,822

Life Expectancy**
United States	77.1 years
Japan	80.7 years
Germany	77.4 years
Mexico	71.5 years
Iran	69.7 years
Nigeria	51.6 years

Gross Domestic Product** (GDP)
United States	$9.3 trillion
Japan	$3.0 trillion
Germany	$1.9 trillion
Mexico	$865.5 billion
Iran	$347.6 billion
Nigeria	$110.5 billion ('99)

Unemployment*
United States	4.2%
Japan	4.7%
Germany	10.5%
Mexico	2.5%***
Iran	25.0%
Nigeria	28.0% ('92)

Per Capita Income*
United States	$33,900
Japan	$23,400
Germany	$22,700
Mexico	$8,500
Iran	$5,300
Nigeria	$970

Defense Spending*
United States	$276.7 billion (3.2% of GDP)
Japan	$42.9 billion (0.9% of GDP)
Germany	$32.8 billion (1.5% of GDP)
Mexico	$4 billion (1% of '99 GDP)
Iran	$5.8 billion (2.9% of GDP)
Nigeria	$236 million (.7% of GDP)

*1999
**2000
***1998 urban rate; plus considerable underemployment
Source: *The World Factbook 2000*, published by the CIA

nuclear arsenal was equaled only by that of the United States. Yet by the late 1980s, the Soviet economy was on the verge of collapse, causing discontent among the peoples of the various Soviet republics. By late 1991, the Soviet Union, a country that had the nuclear capability to destroy the world ten times over, had disintegrated. Although a number of factors contributed to the breakup, most experts agree that the chaotic state of the economy triggered the anger of the people, which escalated into a nationwide protest against the communist government.

MILITARY POWER

Although most experts believe that today a country's power and security are determined more by the size of its gross domestic product than by the size of its army, a strong military is still an important factor in a nation's pursuit of power and the direction of its foreign policy.

For example, if a country is under threat of invasion, its army, not its economy, will deter attack. In 1990, Kuwait, a small but rich oil-producing Middle Eastern country, was unable to mount a strong defense against invasion by Iraq, which at that time had the fourth-largest army in the world. And it was the military power of the United States that led the allied effort to oust Iraq from Kuwait six months later. Likewise, when Serbian troops invaded Kosovo in 1999, forces belonging to the North Atlantic Treaty Organization (NATO) came to the aid of the small and ill-equipped Kosovo Liberation Army. After NATO bombed Serbian targets for seventy-eight days, Serbian president Slobodan Milosevic withdrew his troops. The Persian Gulf War and the conflict in Kosovo proved that military strength in the post–Cold War world is still vital in providing power and influence to many nations and bringing stability to the world.

Sometimes a nation will try to compensate for its economic weakness by building its military strength. Since the end of the Cold War, a number of countries with weak economies—including North Korea, Iran, Iraq, Pakistan, India, and Libya—have drawn worldwide concern by starting programs to build or acquire nuclear weapons. Through threats, sanctions, and negotiations, the United States and other countries have worked to prevent these nations from developing weapons programs. They fear that the leadership in several of these nations is too unpredictable to be trusted with such destructive power. Some experts also believe that if one nation acquires a nuclear arsenal, its neighbors will do likewise, thereby threatening the security of an entire region.

The United States is the most powerful military presence on Earth; it also has the strongest economy. This combination gives the United States unparalleled influence in global affairs. The United States still uses its formidable military to solve armed conflicts around the world. However, since the end of the Cold War, the focus of U.S. foreign policy has been on building economic partnerships with other countries. For instance, in 2000, Congress voted to grant permanent normal trade relations (PNTR) to China—a country with a large military and an emerging economy. Many foreign policy analysts believe that this will be an effective and profitable way to preserve national security because countries with economic ties are less likely to engage each other in armed conflict.

GEOGRAPHY

Geopolitics—the influence of geography and demographics on foreign policy—plays an important role in determining a country's economic and military strength.

Nations that control a resource—such as oil—can wield considerable influence in the world.

Size is an important geopolitical characteristic of every nation. Large nations have advantages over small ones. First, large countries are more likely to contain important mineral resources, fertile soil, diverse terrain, and a variety of climates. These conditions allow a nation to create a *diversified economy*—an economy that is not dependent on a single crop or industry. For example, American farmers can produce a variety of crops and livestock that require different types of soil and growing seasons. U.S. manufacturers can choose from a variety of *natural resources*—such as coal, oil, natural gas, timber, and minerals—that allow them to develop a wide range of industries and products. Economic diversity is important because nations that center their economies on only one commodity are vulnerable to poor harvests and fluctuations in world markets.

Climate and terrain are additional factors that affect the geopolitics of a nation. Many African countries do not receive sufficient rainfall to grow enough food for their populations. Thus, leaders of these countries must cultivate good relations with other nations that can provide them with adequate food.

The terrain along a nation's borders can affect that nation's security. For example, Kuwait was easily overrun by Iraq's army in 1990 in part because the border between the two nations is a desert plain that offers no natural protection. By contrast, Austria is protected in part by the Alps mountains on its western and southern borders.

Some nations lacking size and population can nonetheless command considerable influence in the world if they control a resource that is in great demand. For example, oil-producing countries in the Middle East have traditionally wielded significant influence in the world because the economies of many Western nations, including the United States, are greatly dependent on oil.

MODERN TECHNOLOGY

Countries may be able to overcome their small size and population and scarce natural resources by developing and acquiring modern technology. Indeed, many believe that today, technology—aerospace, telecommunications, and microelectronics—is the dominant factor in determining a country's ability to compete economically and militarily. In many parts of the world, technological innovation is crucial to economic and social development and is an essential ingredient in a country's standard of living. Technology is used in virtually every facet of a country's daily existence—from improving communication and education to building roads and highways. Technology also allows developing countries to catch up and compete with wealthier nations.

Technological innovation is the common thread that runs through the advanced industrialized economies in the United States, the European Union, and Japan. After World War II, the United States was the technological leader of the world—a position that diminished as Japan and Europe improved their economies during the 1950s and 1960s. Their governments spent billions of dollars on research and development of new technologies. Japan's huge investment in research and development had established the country, which has few natural resources, as a leading economic power by the mid-1970s. Japan's domination of the microelectronics market is a major reason its economy has thrived.

Military technology has been a driving force in international relations in the twentieth century. Many experts believe that the creation of the nuclear bomb was the most important technological development of the century; the bomb's presence in the world controlled many foreign policy decisions of U.S. and Soviet leaders. In addition, advances in military hardware have revolutionized warfare. Troop size is no match for the kind of sophisticated military technology that allowed the United States to overrun Iraq's huge army during the Persian Gulf War. Technological innovations also minimized the risk of NATO fatalities during the Kosovo conflict because pilots were able to accurately bomb Serbian troops from high altitudes. While NATO reported that more than 5,000 members of the Yugoslav security force were killed in the bombing, NATO did not suffer a single combat death.

NATIONAL RESOLVE

Even without geographic advantages or technological expertise, a nation can achieve some of its goals if its people share strong beliefs about their national interests and a strong desire to achieve them. This important, though intangible, element of power is known as *national resolve*.

Often, the political leaders of a nation mobilize public opinion and motivate people to work together to achieve their nation's goals. Throughout history, appeals to nationalism or ideology have prompted people to sacrifice for the good of the nation. Threats to national security also increase resolve. For example, Iranian soldiers killed during the Iran-Iraq war in the 1980s were considered religious martyrs in Iran. Inspired by Islamic teachings, these young soldiers were willing to die for their country's cause. Israel's national resolve has played a major role over the years in defending against attacks from neighboring Arab countries.

Post–World War II Japan is an example of how national resolve helped rebuild a nation into a global

Taiwanese companies are among the world's leaders in manufacturing computer chips and computer equipment.

World War II left the Japanese city of Hiroshima, and much of the country, in ruins. However, in the following decades, the Japanese people's strong national resolve helped to reconstruct the country and transform it into a global power.

economic power. The Japanese people were determined to rebuild their nation after the war. During the 1950s and 1960s, the will of the Japanese people to succeed helped repair their country's industrial base and infrastructure, which led to Japan's emergence as a global economic power in the late 1970s.

Geography, modern technology, and national resolve play major roles in contributing to a nation's economic and military success. For these reasons, leaders seek to convert the advantages of their nation into power and influence abroad.

1.3 THE TOOLS OF FOREIGN POLICY

Nations possess an array of tools for carrying out foreign policy goals. Diplomacy, foreign aid, and military intervention are examples. Some tools, although they do not directly involve the military, are so severe that they are considered equivalent to war. When formulating foreign policy, a nation's leaders must consider not only their own goals, but also how other countries will be affected. An effective leader anticipates the reaction of other nations and uses the foreign policy tools that are appropriate to the situation.

DIPLOMACY

Diplomatic relations are the formal contacts between national governments. Most of the business between nations is conducted through discussions and conferences involving diplomats. Diplomats arrange trade and shipping agreements and serve as resource people for visiting citizens. To avoid unnecessary disagreements, diplomacy is conducted under strict international rules and conventions.

Ambassadors are the highest-ranking diplomats. They customarily reside in their assigned country, where they represent the opinions and interests of their own country and report home on major developments in the host country.

Diplomatic Recognition

By establishing diplomatic relations, one nation recognizes, or accepts, the right of another government to represent its people. Nations use diplomatic recognition to express approval or disapproval of another nation's new government. If a nation approves of a new government, it will recognize that government and exchange ambassadors. If a nation disapproves of the government, it will withhold or withdraw diplomatic recognition and not conduct formal relations.

The United Nations was formed in 1945 to promote global peace. It also provides a forum for member countries to discuss their national interests and express their opinions about problems affecting nations around the world.

Recalling Diplomats

When a nation disapproves of the actions of another nation, it may choose to change or suspend its diplomatic relationship with the offending country. For example, during one of NATO's air strikes against Serbia in 1999, three U.S. satellite-guided bombs mistakenly struck the Chinese embassy in the capital of Belgrade, killing three diplomats and wounding twenty more. Chinese government officials condemned U.S. actions by temporarily suspending negotiations with the United States on human rights, arms control, and international security issues.

When one nation strongly disapproves of another nation's policies, the displeased nation may recall its diplomats and order them to return home. However, the recalling of diplomats is considered an extreme measure. Sometimes only the ambassador is recalled, in which case day-to-day relations between nations, although strained, can continue. When all diplomats are recalled, it signals a complete cutoff of diplomatic relations.

Expelling Diplomats

Under international law, diplomats and their families cannot be arrested or tried for a crime in the host nation. This practice, known as *diplomatic immunity*, was developed to protect diplomats from harsh treatment if two nations are at war or on bad terms. However, diplomats can be expelled by the host country. A host government usually orders expulsions when it strongly disagrees with the policies of another country or when a diplomat commits a serious crime such as spying. Nations often respond to these expulsions by expelling the other nation's diplomats as well.

Cultural and Scientific Exchanges

When nations wish to extend goodwill to each other, they sometimes arrange cultural and scientific exchanges. For example, groups of scientists may travel from one country to another to share information, or nations may arrange visits from painters, dance troupes, and musicians to share their different cultures with one another.

Negotiations and Treaties

When conflicts arise between two or more nations, government officials usually hold talks to try to resolve the problem peacefully. At such talks, officials exchange information, discuss the views of their leaders, and try to negotiate solutions. Officials often formalize solutions by writing a *treaty*. Bilateral treaties are formal agreements between two nations. Multilateral treaties are treaties signed by three or more nations.

Treaties form the basis of international law and cover a variety of issues including the handling of international law, coordination of international air traffic, regulation of nuclear tests, and cooperation on plans to protect the environment.

Summits

Most negotiations among nations are conducted by high-ranking diplomats and other officials. However, sometimes an issue is so important that heads of state need to talk face to face. Meetings between heads of state are called *summits*. Summits attempt to create cooperation among nations, most often to resolve immediate problems but sometimes to lay the groundwork for improving longer-term or broader relations. In June 2000, the leaders of North and South Korea met at a summit that many people think may mark the beginning of a friendlier relationship between the two countries. At the summit, the leaders discussed reconciliation and eventual reunification; the reunion of families separated when Korea was divided; and future economic, social, and cultural exchanges.

In June 2000, North Korean leader Kim Jong-II and South Korean president Kim Jae-Dung met at a summit to ease tensions and to lay the groundwork for the countries' future reunification.

TRADE RELATIONS

Trade has become an extremely important tool of foreign policy. Some trade agreements are made between nations to reduce or eliminate trade restrictions on each other's goods. This type of agreement is designed to promote stability and growth in the economies of both nations.

Nations can also use trade to try to change or influence the domestic policies of a trading partner. Restrictions on trade can be instituted to show disapproval of a nation's policies. Trade relations often reflect the state of political relations between nations.

Establishing Trade Relations

Establishing trade relations is one way of showing cooperation between nations after a period of tension. For example, in 2000, leaders from the United States and Vietnam signed an agreement to open trade relations in an effort to speed reconciliation between the former enemies.

In addition, trade relations allow nations to open up communications while they work out political differences. The United States' trade relationship with China gives U.S. policymakers an avenue of communication through which they can pressure Chinese leaders to improve the Chinese government's human rights record.

Restrictions on Trade

Protectionism is the use of trade restrictions to protect a domestic market from foreign imports or to discriminate against products exported by another nation. Trade restrictions, or trade barriers, take two basic forms—tariffs and quotas. *Tariffs* are taxes on imports. *Quotas* set limits on the amount of goods that can be imported.

Because commerce between nations is so important in today's global economy, fewer nations now practice protectionism than in the past. When a country misses out on the jobs and cashflow that foreign trade and investments can bring, it risks losing more than it could gain through protecting its domestic industries.

Trade Agreements

Countries sign trade agreements to gain access to another country's market. Such treaties can be used to reduce or eliminate trade barriers and to stimulate trade in new goods and services. The General Agreement on Tariffs and Trade (GATT) is a multilateral—involving more than two countries—trade agreement. Nations that have signed the GATT periodically agree to negotiate new rules, lower tariffs, and lessen trade restrictions to help increase trade worldwide. The last GATT agreement was signed in 1994.

FOREIGN AID

Many of the world's wealthy nations provide economic and military aid to other countries to foster economic development, gain and protect allies, and promote internal stability. *Foreign aid* can come in the form of cash, equipment, or technical advice. Aid falls into two categories: economic and military.

Economic Aid

Economic aid is usually given in the form of cash grants or loans, but it can also include food, agricultural equipment, or technical assistance. Developing nations use economic aid for a wide variety of improvements, including road construction, electrification projects, agricultural reform, and the development of domestic industries. Economic aid can also be used to find long-term solutions to overpopulation, hunger, or disease.

Nations seek economic aid from international organizations, such as the World Bank, or from individual countries. Aid that is granted through an international organization to which many nations contribute is called *multilateral aid*. Aid that is granted by one nation directly to another nation is called *bilateral aid*.

Military Aid

Military aid often consists of cash grants for developing a stronger defense but can also include weapons, training programs, or military advisers. Military aid serves to enhance the donor nation's security by strengthening another nation's military forces. Military aid is used to help friendly governments stay in power or to aid potential allies in their efforts to overthrow a hostile government. For example, in 2000, the U.S. Congress approved a $1.3 billion aid package targeted at strengthening and modernizing the Colombian military.

ALLIANCES

Alliances are multilateral agreements among nations to protect each other in case of attack by an adversary. Nations join together in military alliances for mutual protection and support of common interests. By joining together, nations tend to have more power—both militarily and politically. For this reason, alliances are especially important to smaller nations.

The most powerful military alliance today is the North Atlantic Treaty Organization (NATO). Formed in 1949, NATO now includes Belgium, Canada, the Czech Republic, Denmark, France, Germany, Greece, Hungary, Iceland, Italy, Luxembourg, the Netherlands, Norway, Poland, Portugal, Spain, Turkey, the United Kingdom, and the United States. Under the NATO agreement, nations consider an attack on any member country of the alliance as an attack on all members.

INTERNATIONAL AND REGIONAL ORGANIZATIONS

International organizations are made up of every nation that wishes to participate. Regional organizations consist of nations in one particular area of the world. These organizations vary greatly in purpose and in the types of issues they address. International and regional organizations play a dual role in international relations. First, they provide a forum for addressing problems that affect all nations, and second, they act as "players" in the international arena themselves. However, international cooperation sometimes breaks down because individual nations use these organizations to pursue their own national interests.

International Organizations

The United Nations (UN) is the most prominent international organization. Its primary purpose is to promote peace. For more powerful countries, the United Nations provides a forum to discuss their different national interests. For smaller countries, the United Nations provides an equal opportunity to express their views—regardless of their size, population, economic development, or military strength.

There are numerous other international organizations that are devoted to a variety of purposes. These include the World Health Organization, the International Monetary Fund, the World Bank, and the International Atomic Energy Agency.

Regional Organizations

Regional organizations operate much like international organizations, except that their members are located in a particular region of the world. For example, the European Union (EU) is composed of most western European nations and may soon include eastern European nations. The European Union promotes economic cooperation among its members by lowering tariffs and encouraging intra-European trade. The Organization of American States (OAS) was established to promote the joint interests of the sovereign nations of North America and South America and to provide for the collective security of these nations. Other regional organizations, such as the Organization of Petroleum Exporting Countries (OPEC), were founded so that smaller nations could compete with the superpowers on economic and political issues. The Southern African Development Community (SADC) is an example of a regional organization formed to reduce poverty and promote economic stability, trade, and democracy in developing countries. Working together, these nations are stronger than they would be if they functioned alone.

In 2000, the United States approved a $1.3 billion military aid package to assist Colombia in its fight against rebels controlling much of the country's drug trade. Some of the money will go to help destroy drug crops and drug-producing facilities. Here, a Colombian antinarcotics police officer guards a burning cocaine lab.

BOYCOTTS AND SANCTIONS

Boycotts and sanctions are hostile actions taken against nations. These measures are the most severe form of action that can be taken against a nation short of military action. In some circumstances, boycotts and sanctions are considered acts of war.

A *boycott* is a decision by one nation or a group of nations to abstain from buying certain goods to try to force a particular nation to change its policies. Boycotts may also take the form of a refusal to participate in international events or meetings. For example, the United States boycotted the 1980 summer Olympic games in Moscow to protest the Soviet Union's invasion of Afghanistan.

A *sanction* is an action taken by one or more nations to force another nation to comply with international law or to change its policies. The most common and severe sanctions are economic sanctions. Sanctions are controversial, partly because they are not consistently effective in forcing countries to change their policies. One of the most effective uses of sanctions, however, was in South Africa. For more than 40 years, South Africa was governed under the apartheid system, which upheld official racial segregation. Over the years, condemnation of this system grew in the international community, which responded with economic and arms sanctions. By the late 1980s, the sanctions, combined with antiapartheid protests within South Africa, finally forced the government to dismantle apartheid.

PROPAGANDA

Propaganda is one-sided or exaggerated information used by a nation to gain both national and international support for its policies or to discredit the policies of an adversary. Propaganda is spread through newspapers, books, film, radio, and television. Throughout history, propaganda has been used extensively to influence public opinion.

MILITARY FORCE

For centuries, people have used military force to gain territory, reclaim previously lost land, extend power over another group of people, spread a religion, or settle disputes. If diplomacy fails to resolve a conflict, or a nation perceives that there are no other alternatives, nations may resort to using military force.

Yet war is only one way that nations use military force in support of foreign policy. Some uses of a

A SHIFTING VIEW OF SANCTIONS

As world economies have become increasingly intertwined, the incentive for countries to engage in armed conflict has decreased. Nations have more to lose economically if they cannot depend on international trade. Consequently, the use of economic sanctions over military force to achieve change has become more appealing to world leaders, especially U.S. leaders. Under the Clinton administration, the United States government imposed more economic sanctions than at any other time in history.

However, the use of sanctions is controversial. Many experts believe that they are rarely effective in forcing countries to change their policies and often backfire by isolating sanctioned countries and causing their leaders to become even more repressive. Humanitarian groups say that economic sanctions are unfair and cruel because they punish civilians. For example, some humanitarian activists claim that in Iraq, U.S. sanctions that deny food and medicine to the country have resulted in the deaths of 1.2 million people, mostly children and the elderly. The heads of U.S. farms and businesses also complain that U.S. sanctions against other countries hurt them by cutting the markets in which they can sell their products.

In response to these complaints and to changes in world politics, the United States has begun to relax or lift some of its economic sanctions. Recently, North Korea, Cuba, Iran, Libya, and Yugoslavia have all benefited from a more flexible U.S. policy regarding sanctions. In the case of some of these countries, sanctions have been lifted as a reward for policy changes. For example, because North Korea agreed to stop testing its long-range missiles, the United States decided to drop barriers blocking the trade of most U.S. and North Korean consumer goods and to relax transportation restrictions between the two countries. In general, the prevalent attitude among U.S. lawmakers is that sanctions should be applied with more care and consideration to make them an effective—and humane—foreign policy tool.

nation's military are meant simply as warnings. Others represent a challenge to another nation's sovereignty. Still other military uses are direct threats to another nation's security. When a nation's leaders contemplate using military force, they often consider the consequences of their actions and try to anticipate the reactions of their adversaries and of the world community.

Show of Strength

Nations maintain military forces to show that they are prepared to defend themselves. One way to show strength is to strategically position armed forces around the world.

If a nation perceives that a conflict in another region of the world may threaten its national interest, it may send part of its military forces to that region. In this way, a nation can monitor a situation. For example, when Iraqi armed forces moved close to the Kuwaiti border in 1994, the United States dispatched 40,000 troops to Kuwait to ward off another possible invasion. Iraqi forces pulled back days later. Some U.S. troops remain stationed in Kuwait to guard against another invasion.

Terrorism

Terrorism involves acts of violence or destruction—such as hijacking airplanes, taking hostages, or setting off bombs in public places—that are carried out by nongovernmental groups that want to gain attention for their political causes. Sometimes these groups receive equipment, money, or moral support from their own or foreign governments. Although most countries condemn terrorism, some nations support it, usually secretly, to help accomplish foreign policy goals that seem difficult to achieve in other ways.

Many experts say that the world may witness new forms of terrorism in the twenty-first century. Some fear that terrorists will be able to use computers to secretly attack other countries from a distance. For example, an increased reliance on computers and the Internet may help make systems at water purification and power plants run more efficiently, but it also leaves them vulnerable to attack by computer hackers.

Limited Military Response

Limited military responses are short-term military actions designed to force another nation to back down in a specific dispute and possibly to resolve the conflict through diplomacy. A limited military response warns the offending nation that it is risking full-scale war by its actions and alerts the world community that a nation is willing to fight for its security and ideals. The action clearly communicates what a nation considers unacceptable. In 1998, in response to terrorist bombings of the U.S. embassies in Tanzania and Kenya, American aircraft bombed targets in Sudan and Afghanistan—nations suspected of harboring Osama bin Laden, the mastermind behind the embassy bombings. Through this limited military response, the United States let the world know that it would not tolerate terrorist attacks against American citizens.

War

When all efforts for solving a conflict fail, nations go to war. Because the costs of war—to individuals, to society, and to nations—are tremendous, most nations perceive war as the foreign policy tool of last resort. Most countries go to war only when they believe that its benefits will outweigh its significant costs.

Chapter Two
How U.S. Foreign Policy Is Made

The national interest of the United States is shaped by many different factors. Like the leaders of other countries, U.S. policymakers seek to develop a foreign policy to protect American citizens, maintain economic and military strength, and preserve the nation's values. In many ways, however, the United States is not like other countries. Its location, economic system, military strength, and type of government have given the United States unique advantages, enabling it to become a key player in world affairs.

However, since the end of the Cold War, American leaders have looked for ways to redefine U.S. foreign policy. From the highest-ranking member of Congress to the average U.S. citizen, everyone has an opinion about what is in the best interest of the United States. Thus, the influences on foreign policy are many. This chapter will address how foreign policy decisions are made and what influences help form those decisions.

2.1 THE UNITED STATES AND THE WORLD

The United States is the leading force in world affairs—militarily, economically, and ideologically—and American interests stretch around the globe. The leaders of the United States place great importance on advancing the cause of freedom in the world. U.S. foreign policy reflects a desire to protect the security of the nation and the security of other democratic nations.

Militarily, the United States is the most powerful country in the world. Having a strong military gives U.S. leaders an important tool in protecting allies, stopping military aggression, and leading international humanitarian missions.

Economically, Americans live in one of the most prosperous nations in the world. The prosperity of the United States stems from its size, variety of climates, and abundance of natural resources. The U.S. economic system of free enterprise allows Americans to take advantage of the opportunities that their nation offers. In large measure, the stability of the United States is directly related to the diversity and strength of its economy.

Ideologically, Americans feel a strong commitment to preserving their way of life. They live in one of the world's freest societies. Their system of government guarantees them the right to think, speak, worship, and act freely upon their own beliefs.

Some historians call the twentieth century the "American century" because the United States exercised unparalleled influence on the political and economic direction of the world. However, most U.S. leaders expect the twenty-first century to be affected more by global partnerships than by a single power. The challenges facing the post–Cold War world require new solutions and new policies. Accordingly, the United States has had to adapt its foreign policy to fit a changing and complex world.

2.2 "AN INVITATION TO STRUGGLE": THE PRESIDENT AND CONGRESS

Developing priorities and strategies for the United States' role in the world has not been easy. The U.S. Constitution divides the power to determine foreign policy between the president and Congress. This division makes policy development more difficult. Since the founding of the United States, the executive and legislative branches have fought with each other for control over relations with other countries. In some eras, the president has been dominant, while at other times, Congress has been more powerful. One expert has called the Constitution "an invitation to struggle" over foreign policy.

POWERS OF THE PRESIDENT

The president is the single most important person in the making of foreign policy. The president sets the foreign policy agenda, and Congress must react to it. The most important powers given to the president by the Constitution in regard to foreign policy are the powers to conduct war, to make treaties and other international agreements, and to appoint ambassadors and other top officials.

Conduct War. As commander in chief of all U.S. military forces, the president can use the armed forces to advance U.S. foreign policy goals. Although the Constitution gives Congress the right to declare war, presidents do not need a declaration of war to order the military into battle. For example, the U.S. invasions of Grenada and Panama, in 1983 and 1989, respectively, were ordered by the president without prior approval from Congress.

Since the dawn of the nuclear age, the chief executive has held another awesome responsibility as the commander in chief of the military. Only the president can order a nuclear attack by the United States.

Make Treaties and Other International Agreements. The president and the president's representatives negotiate agreements with other nations to end wars, control weapons, regulate international trade, and resolve other global issues. One type of international agreement, a treaty, must be submitted to the Senate for approval before it can go into effect. However, in recent years, presidents frequently have used executive agreements, international accords that do not require Senate approval. Such agreements allow presidents and their advisers to work out agreements with other governments without having to seek the Senate's approval.

Appoint Ambassadors and Other Top Officials. It is important for presidents to be represented by people who agree with their general approach to foreign policy. In addition to appointments made in recognition of particular expertise, presidents often reward individuals who supported their election campaigns by appointing them to be ambassadors.

PRESIDENTIAL DECISIONMAKING

Although the president is the ultimate decisionmaker, the responsibility for gathering information and offering advice is delegated to the many cabinet members, advisers, and other government officials who work for the chief executive.

The White House Staff. The president, as chief executive, is surrounded by personal aides who help the president sort through many competing demands. They advise the chief executive on the political and economic consequences of foreign policy decisions. The vice president may be an important adviser to the president and frequently represents the White House on official visits to other countries.

The National Security Council (NSC) is the group within the White House that coordinates foreign policy. Chaired by the president, it is the body that commonly shapes the U.S. response to a foreign policy crisis.

The Cabinet. Outside the White House, the two most important agencies in determining foreign policy are the Department of State and the Department of Defense. These cabinet departments are headed by secretaries appointed by the president.

The secretary of state, as the United States' top diplomat, travels around the world to meet with world leaders, discuss issues and problems, and negotiate agreements. The secretary of defense supervises the operations of the U.S. military and advises the president of the practicality of military action to solve disputes with other nations.

The Bureaucracy. The government bureaucracy consists of the many offices and administrations set up to carry out the president's policies. Most bureaucrats are

Although the president of the United States is the commander in chief of all U.S. military forces, the Constitution gives the power to declare war to Congress. Here, President Franklin Roosevelt signs a congressional declaration of war against Japan, launching the United States into World War II.

civil service employees who stay with the government regardless of changes in presidential administrations. The most important foreign policy bureaucracy is the Foreign Service, the corps of professional diplomats who hold positions in embassies abroad. These officials are supposed to support the policies of the current administration. However, diplomats sometimes disagree personally with those policies and may seek to alter or delay the course favored by the president in hopes that the next president will adopt a different policy. During such instances, supporters of the president frequently complain that permanent foreign policy bureaucrats do not work hard enough to carry out the administration's policies.

Intelligence Agencies. The president has access to important intelligence information. Intelligence agencies—such as the Central Intelligence Agency (CIA), the Defense Intelligence Agency (DIA), and the National Security Agency (NSA)—provide information to the president that is not available to Congress.

Intelligence agencies are responsible for evaluating the strength of another country's military force and for predicting what other countries intend to do. Intelligence agencies undertake secret spying operations and analyze publicly available information. In addition, they may be asked to engage in covert, or secret, actions: missions that U.S. leaders do not want to be identified with publicly, but which they believe are necessary for the success of a particular policy objective.

POWERS OF CONGRESS

The Constitution gives Congress a number of ways to influence foreign policy. Under the Constitution, Congress has the power to declare war, control spending, approve treaties, confirm presidential nominations, and pass laws or resolutions stating a specific policy.

Declare War. Although the Constitution puts the president in charge of military operations, it gives Congress the right to place the nation in a formal state of war. However, this right has become less important over the years because presidents have ordered military action without asking Congress to declare war. The last

---

THE MAKING OF AMERICAN FOREIGN POLICY

The President
- Makes foreign policy decisions
- Is commander in chief of the military
- Makes executive agreements

Department of Defense
- Advises the president (secretary and joint chiefs of staff)
- Implements policy decisions and military orders
- Maintains nation's armed forces
- Oversees military aid to other countries

Central Intelligence Agency (CIA)
- Advises the president and National Security Council (director)
- Gathers and analyzes information
- Carries out special covert operations

Department of State
- Advises the president and acts as the nation's chief diplomat (secretary)
- Implements policy decisions
- Conducts relations with other countries (embassies)
- Administers foreign aid

National Security Council (NSC)
- Advises the president
- Coordinates policymaking and implementation
- Conducts major policy studies
- Includes as its statutory members: president, vice president, secretary of state, secretary of defense

Other Executive Agencies
These bodies include:
- Department of Agriculture
- Department of Commerce
- Department of the Treasury
- Arms Control and Disarmament Agency
- United States Information Agency
- Peace Corps

time Congress actually declared war was in 1941 against Japan and Germany. However, on occasion, Congress has given the president formal authorization—without actually declaring war—to use military force on another country. For example, in 1964, Congress passed the Tonkin Gulf Resolution, which authorized President Lyndon Johnson to "deter further aggression" from the North Vietnamese in Vietnam. Only once since World War II has Congress specifically given the president approval to wage war on another country. In January 1991, the legislative branch gave President George Bush formal authorization to use U.S. armed forces to oust Iraq from Kuwait.

In 1973, Congress passed the War Powers Act as a way to establish limits on presidential use of the armed forces. Under this law, the president is allowed to commit U.S. troops to battle for only sixty days. To go beyond that time, the president must persuade Congress to pass a resolution supporting continued use of troops.

Control Spending. The Constitution gives Congress "the power of the purse." Congress has used that power in recent years to influence foreign policy by providing—or refusing to provide—funds for programs supported by the president. For example, during the early 1970s, members of Congress who opposed the war in Vietnam sought to cut off funds for continuation of U.S. actions.

Foreign aid is one of the most frequent targets of Congress's power to control spending. For many years, some senators and representatives have complained about foreign aid, arguing that money given to other governments would be better spent at home or in countries that currently receive little or no U.S. aid. Congress frequently acts to reduce the president's requests for both military and economic foreign aid.

Approve Treaties and Confirm Presidential Nominations. The Constitution gives the power to approve treaties and the power to confirm presidential nominations only to the Senate, not to the House of Representatives. Treaties must be ratified, or approved, by two-thirds of the Senate. However, the Senate's right to advise and give consent to the president in making treaties has become less important in recent decades. Presidents have made many executive agreements rather than formal treaties to avoid having to seek Senate approval on their international agreements.

The Senate rarely rejects a treaty outright, but it can amend treaties. Fewer than two dozen treaties have been defeated in the nation's history. In 1999, the Senate voted not to approve the Comprehensive Test

Since the founding of the nation, the executive and legislative branches have fought each other for control over U.S. foreign policy. Here, President Harry Truman appeals to a joint session of Congress to allot more money and resources to fight communism.

Ban Treaty (CTBT), which was supported by the Clinton administration. If opposition to a treaty is strong, the president may elect to withdraw it from Senate consideration rather than risk political defeat. In 1979, President Jimmy Carter withdrew Strategic Arms Limitations Talks II (SALT II), an arms control agreement with the Soviet Union, from Senate consideration because of mounting opposition.

Confirming the president's appointment of foreign policy officials is another power of the Senate. In some cases, members of the Senate may oppose a nomination as a way of criticizing the president's policies.

Pass Laws or Resolutions Stating a Specific Policy. The Constitution grants Congress the power to pass legislation directing the president on foreign policy matters. Such direction can range from simple expressions of congressional opinion (such as instructing the president in 1993 not to place U.S. armed forces under the command of the United Nations) to detailed blueprints for foreign aid programs (such as making payment of U.S. dues to the United Nations dependent on the UN's agreement to implement internal reforms in 1999).

Sometimes, however, Congress will try to pressure the president into changing a policy. In 1994, many members of Congress became frustrated with the Clinton administration's policy toward the conflict in Bosnia-Herzegovina. Many lawmakers believed that the United Nations arms embargo on the war-torn country prevented Bosnian Muslims from defending themselves. President Bill Clinton was hesitant to lift the embargo because he believed such an action would escalate the war and drag American soldiers into the conflict. In July 1995, the House of Representatives and the Senate voted to lift unilaterally the arms embargo on Bosnia. However, President Clinton vetoed the measure.

THE PRESIDENT VS. CONGRESS

Constitutional Powers: Foreign Policy

The President
- Conduct war
- Negotiate treaties and other international agreements
- Appoint ambassadors and other top officials

Congress
- Declare war
- Control spending
- Approve treaties and confirm presidential nominations
- Pass laws or resolutions stating a specific policy

CONGRESSIONAL DECISIONMAKING

Congress deals with foreign policy issues quite differently than the executive branch does. Unlike the executive branch—where one person, the president, has the final authority over all decisions—power in Congress is spread out. Many different congressional committees can affect foreign policy. Decisionmaking in Congress can be slow and cumbersome, and many members think the legislative process is ill suited to the rapid changes that take place in international relations.

Two committees, the Senate Foreign Relations Committee and the House Foreign Affairs Committee, have formal authority over foreign policy issues. However, the prestige and power of those two panels have lessened in recent years as other committees have asserted influence over important foreign policy issues. For example, the House and Senate Armed Services Committees can influence arms negotiations and decisions to make military commitments to other countries.

Congressional committees hold hearings to examine an administration's foreign policy programs. During these hearings, members of the administration answer questions and explain the president's policies.

of the 535 members of Congress has his or her own ideas about how foreign policy should be conducted. Individual members of Congress often seek to influence foreign policy by mobilizing public support for their views.

The House Ways and Means Committee and the Senate Finance Committee can affect international trade by approving legislation to raise or lower tariffs. Members of Congress can also call for special hearings to examine the administration's foreign policy programs. Congressional hearings are sometimes used as a forum to criticize a president or a policy. In 1987, the House and Senate got together for a joint foreign policy hearing to probe the Reagan administration's policy in Central America, particularly the administration's policies supporting the Nicaraguan rebel group known as the *contras*.

Traditionally, members of Congress have tried to put aside party differences and present a common front when dealing with other countries. Members frequently say that politics stop at the water's edge. However, each

2.3 OTHER INFLUENCES ON FOREIGN POLICY

The president, top White House advisers, and members of Congress are not the only people who play a role in determining U.S. foreign policy. Many individuals and institutions outside the government are vitally concerned with how the United States acts in the international arena. In many cases, these groups are able to pressure government officials to adopt their positions on foreign policy. The president and Congress must consider these outside influences when making foreign policy decisions.

PUBLIC OPINION

The opinions of the American people play a significant role in affecting how the United States relates to other countries. Public opinion most often is expressed through organized groups of people who seek to lobby, or persuade, government officials to support a particular point of view. These groups organize around single issues or broad political philosophies.

For example, some groups support a single issue. The American Israel Public Affairs Committee works to maintain and improve relations between the United States and Israel. Other organizations work on broader foreign policy issues. Greenpeace works to prevent the disposal of hazardous waste around the world; to protect marine mammals in the oceans; and to preserve Antarctica as a world park, free from industry, military development, and nuclear power. These interest groups seek to influence foreign policy by educating members of Congress and the public about their views and by contributing time and money to elect officials who support their positions.

Another type of group that affects foreign policy is composed of Americans who feel ties of blood and loyalty to the countries in which they were born. Such ethnic groups sometimes have a major effect on U.S. foreign policy. For example, many people in the Cuban-American community in Miami, Florida,

Groups of Americans with ethnic roots in other countries often influence U.S. foreign policy. Here, members of Miami's Cuban-American community protest the U.S. government's decision to return Elian Gonzalez to his father's custody.

HOW U.S. FOREIGN POLICY IS MADE 33

strongly support using the U.S. trade embargo with Cuba to force military dictator Fidel Castro into allowing Cuban citizens more freedom.

Americans who are not members of special interest organizations can influence foreign policy by voting. In times of crisis, events in other countries can influence the outcome of an election. For example, in 1968, Richard Nixon was elected president in large part because he promised to end the Vietnam War. Many people believe that President Jimmy Carter failed to win reelection in 1980 because he was unable to secure a quick release of the American hostages in Iran.

As leaders seek policies that are in the long-term best interests of the nation as a whole, they must consider the competing views of many different segments of American society.

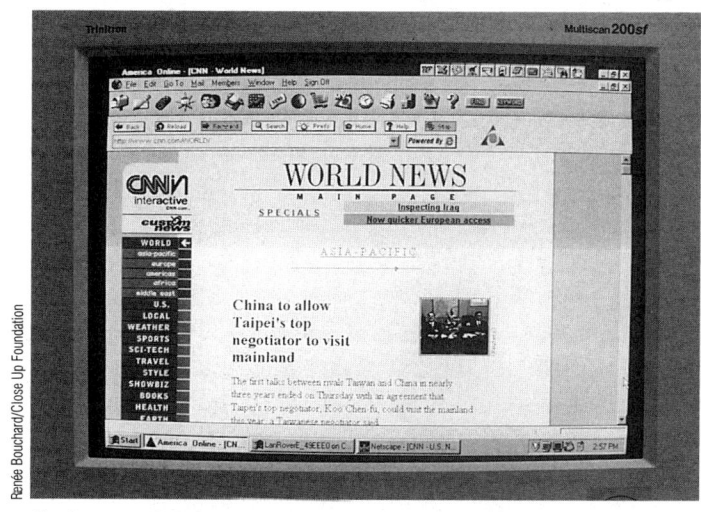

The Internet offers Americans greater access to news from around the world.

THE MEDIA

Most Americans receive information about foreign policy issues from the mass media: television, radio, newspapers, newsmagazines, and the Internet. For this reason, the way the media cover an issue can influence public opinion and the direction of U.S. foreign policy. U.S. leaders must consider how their actions will be interpreted by the press. Leaders in a democracy must keep in mind media coverage—whether balanced or biased, shallow or thorough—and its effect on public opinion.

Because it can present events so vividly, television has an especially strong effect on public opinion about foreign policy issues. During the Vietnam War, television news cameras followed U.S. fighting forces into battle and gave most viewers their first glimpse of the sights and sounds of war. Faced with vivid images of death and destruction, many Americans became convinced that the war was a mistake, and they pressed the president and Congress to end U.S. involvement in Vietnam.

In 1999, television networks extensively covered the crisis in Kosovo. Americans saw moving footage of Serbs forcing ethnic Albanians out of their homes and into refugee camps across the Kosovar border. These images helped convince Americans that the NATO decision to intervene in Kosovo and bomb Serbian targets was the right and necessary choice.

Television coverage of African disasters such as the famine in Ethiopia in the late 1980s has also galvanized U.S. support for increasing disaster relief to countries there. However, some people say that in the long run, media coverage of Africa has had a negative effect on the public's opinion of the continent. These observers believe that because the media consistently portrays the poverty, famine, civil war, and disease in some African countries as hopeless, Americans are no longer interested in what they perceive as a lost cause.

U.S. ALLIES

The leaders of the United States must seek to balance the wishes of its allies with America's own needs. The U.S. government does not allow its allies to dictate its actions, but neither does it ignore their opinions. American leaders often consult with foreign leaders before making foreign policy decisions.

The most important allies of the United States are the large industrial democracies—Canada, France, Germany, Great Britain, Italy, and Japan. Although the United States also has alliances with many other countries, these countries do not have as much influence on U.S. foreign policy as do these six wealthy and powerful nations.

Often, the United States and its allies do not agree. During the Cold War, the United States and its allies were united around the common goal of containing Soviet expansion. With that threat now gone, there is less to unite the Western world. Consequently, the United States and its allies have faced greater diplomatic obstacles in recent years.

The war in Bosnia was a source of dissension between the United States and Europe. Many experts believe that the inability of the United States and its allies to coordinate a strong, unified plan encouraged the Serbs to continue their military campaign against Bosnia's Muslims. Likewise, the United States and its allies have been unable to reach an agreement on terms governing the creation of an international criminal court to try Yugoslav war criminals. On the other hand, in Kosovo, the U.S.- and European-backed NATO bombing campaign successfully ousted Serbian troops from the territory in less than three months, proving that it is still possible for old friends to work together.

Economic competition between nations can also create tension between allies. For example, in 1998, the World Trade Organization (WTO) ruled that the European Union's ten-year ban on imports of American hormone-treated beef was unjustified. When the EU refused to comply with the WTO decision and continued to ban U.S. beef, the United States responded by imposing 100 percent tariffs intended to double the price of many European food items in the United States. These trade battles hurt food producers in both nations and are an ongoing source of tension between the United States and its European allies.

SEEKING A BALANCE

U.S. foreign policy is shaped by pressures and viewpoints from many different sources. At the center of foreign policy decisionmaking is the president, but he is

In 1999, dramatic news footage of ethnic Albanian civilians fleeing from Serbs in Kosovo helped generate support for the U.S. bombing campaign against Yugoslavia.

THE CHANGING U.S. ROLE IN THE WORLD

During the Cold War, the president and Congress wrestled over whether to use armed forces or offer foreign aid in pursuing their foreign policy goals. Nonetheless, the two branches of government were united over the United States' mission to contain communism. The dangers of the Cold War called for active U.S. engagement in the world.

Today, U.S. leaders grapple with much broader questions about their country's role in the world. They must decide how and where U.S. interests coincide with global interests. Now that there is no immediate threat to U.S. security, many lawmakers and citizens prefer that the United States be more isolated and that policy be centered on domestic issues such as health care reform and crime reduction. The president and Congress also debate whether having the wealthiest economy and strongest military automatically implies that the United States must carry the responsibility for the rest of the world's problems.

What should the criteria be for U.S. military intervention in international conflicts? Many Americans believe that the United States should no longer shoulder the burden of leadership in keeping peace and resolving global crises. While the United States remains an active presence in settling many disputes, it has refused to participate in those not considered important to U.S. national interests—for example, the United States did not participate in the UN peacekeeping mission to East Timor, Indonesia, in 1999. Many Americans believe that the European Union and Japan—each nearly as economically powerful as the United States—should share responsibility for keeping world peace.

Most experts predict that other powerful nations will indeed take on more responsibility in tackling global problems, particularly by sharing the huge financial cost. However, these experts also think that the United States is currently the only nation in the world that has the military and diplomatic muscle to stop armed aggression and broker peace agreements. Some world leaders fear that if the United States were to adopt a more isolationist foreign policy, international crises such as nuclear proliferation, regional conflicts, and terrorism would escalate. UN officials believe that their organization would be ineffective without strong U.S. engagement worldwide. Ultimately, many American leaders say that it is not possible for the United States to isolate itself from the global community because global crises will affect the United States, regardless.

U.S. leaders often consult with their counterparts from other nations before making major foreign policy decisions. U.S. officials attempt to balance the wishes of allied countries with America's own needs. Here, U.S. deputy secretary of state Strobe Talbott is shown at the July 2000 Group of Eight (Russia included) Foreign Ministers meeting in Japan.

closely watched by Congress, the media, voters, and other world leaders. All these players seek to influence foreign policy in a way that they think best satisfies both their interests and the broader national interest.

Different groups exert more influence at different times, pulling national goals and strategies first one way, then another. Presidential elections are held every four years, and a new president's opinions may be substantially different from those of the previous chief executive. For these reasons, U.S. foreign policy is not always consistent from issue to issue, region to region, or president to president.

CHAPTER THREE

THE COLD WAR AND BEYOND

After World War II ended in 1945, the world divided into two blocs: the communist bloc in the East and the democratic bloc in the West. The East, led by the Soviet Union, was composed of authoritarian, communist nations; the West, led by the United States, was democratic and capitalist. These two poles of power engaged in a struggle, known as the Cold War, that defined international relations for the next forty-five years.

By 1991, the Cold War was over, and the West stood alone as the world's military and economic leader. However, no one quite knew what direction the next era of international relations would take. Ten years later, a global system rooted in interdependence, democracy, and shared power has slowly taken shape. Many believe that this new system—although imperfect—is one that can foster economic security and maintain the balance of power in the world.

3.1 THE ORIGINS OF THE COLD WAR

Throughout history, wars have dramatically altered relations among nations. World War II is the classic example. During World War II, Great Britain, the United States, and the Soviet Union put aside differences to defeat the advancing armies of German dictator Adolph Hitler. Nazi Germany threatened the very existence of these three nations. So for almost five years, the ideological separation of nations based on communism and capitalism was replaced with an uneasy alliance.

As the war drew to a close, however, differences in ideology reemerged. Leaders from East and West harbored their own ideas about how to reconstruct Europe. Cooperation dissolved as both sides sought to protect and extend their influence. The end result was the emergence of a world dominated by the United States and the Soviet Union, each with its own sphere of influence.

THE EMERGENCE OF SUPERPOWERS

After the defeat of Nazi Germany and Japan in World War II, the United States became the world's dominant power. The United States had the strongest military force in the world and was the only nation with the atomic bomb. The war had ended the Great Depression, and the U.S. economy had benefited tremendously from the production of wartime materials.

In contrast to the United States, the Soviet Union was devastated by World War II, which left 20 million of its citizens dead and virtually destroyed its countryside.

At the 1945 Yalta Conference in the Crimea, British prime minister Winston Churchill, U.S. president Franklin Roosevelt, and Soviet premier Joseph Stalin began the division of Europe that would shape the Cold War era, partitioning Germany into four occupational zones and granting occupation areas in eastern Europe to the Soviet Union.

Yet Soviet leader Joseph Stalin was eager for his country to assume the role of a world power. The Soviet government was able to rebuild its economy by drawing on its vast natural resources and by confiscating factories in manufacturing centers in eastern Europe, where its huge army remained firmly entrenched. At the same time, the Soviet government accelerated its efforts to build a nuclear arsenal of its own.

Although World War II had strained the resources of all nations involved, the size and vast resources of the United States and the Soviet Union enabled both countries to prosper more quickly than others. No other nation in the world could rival the economic or military power of these two *superpowers*.

"AN IRON CURTAIN HAS DESCENDED"

By 1946, the possibility that the United States and the Soviet Union would cooperate was becoming more remote. Within a matter of weeks after the liberation of eastern Europe from Nazi control, the Soviet Union established communist governments in Poland and Romania. Joseph Stalin viewed eastern Europe as vital to Soviet security. Having been attacked by the Germans twice in thirty years, Soviet leaders sought to set up a "buffer zone" separating Germany from the Soviet Union. As U.S. leaders protested Soviet expansion, Moscow began to view the United States as an enemy and launched a bitter propaganda campaign against it.

In 1946, in a speech delivered in Fulton, Missouri, British prime minister Winston Churchill, with U.S. president Harry Truman at his side, declared, "From Stettin in the Baltic to Trieste in the Adriatic, an iron curtain has descended across the Continent." U.S. leaders believed the Soviet threat to its European allies was a threat to U.S. national security. This action marked a dramatic change in the way the United States perceived its national security. Containing the Soviet Union became the cornerstone of U.S. foreign policy. The Cold War—a war fought with words, not bullets—had begun. Competing ideologies—communism versus capitalism—would dominate international affairs for much of the second half of the twentieth century.

BEGINNING OF THE NUCLEAR ERA

When the United States dropped two atomic bombs on Japan in August 1945 to end World War II, U.S. leaders believed they had a weapon so powerful that it would keep any future adversary at bay. What they did not count on was that the Soviet Union would also develop nuclear weapons soon after the war. In 1949, the Soviet Union tested its first atomic bomb. The nuclear arms race was on.

Over the next four decades, the United States and the Soviet Union competed for nuclear superiority. Technological improvements allowed the superpowers and their allies to develop more powerful weapons that could be delivered with pinpoint accuracy not only from the air, but also from the land and sea.

Both superpowers pursued a policy of *nuclear deterrence*. Deterrence requires each nation to have enough nuclear weapons to survive an attack and still destroy the enemy. Thus, under this strategy, neither nation could launch a nuclear attack without being destroyed by the other. Nuclear deterrence helped fuel the arms race because if one nation improved its weapons, the other side was obliged to match that improvement to maintain balance.

THE COMMITMENT TO EUROPE

In the years following World War II, Europe suffered a severe economic slump. There were shortages of food, housing, and jobs. Governments did not have the resources to provide people with the help they desperately needed. In this charged political climate, communist parties—many of them active in wartime resistance movements—threatened to take control.

In 1947, President Truman announced the Truman Doctrine—a commitment to provide aid to any government fighting communism. In a speech to Congress, Truman asserted, "It must be the policy of the United States to support free peoples who are resisting attempted subjugation by armed minorities or by outside pressures." The Truman Doctrine was part of the wider U.S. strategy, called *containment*, which sought to stop the spread of communism.

At the heart of containment was the commitment to strengthen the economies of U.S. allies in Europe. In 1949, the United States announced a program to provide loans and other types of economic assistance to aid European nations in their economic recovery. The program was called the Marshall Plan. As Secretary of State George Marshall stated, "Our policy is directed not against any country or doctrine but against hunger, poverty, desperation, and chaos."

Through the Marshall Plan, the United States provided $12.5 billion in economic and military aid to western Europe. By 1951, Europe's industrial output exceeded its prewar rate by 40 percent. The Marshall Plan helped to reduce the power of communist parties in western Europe by strengthening existing governments.

Thus, the division of Europe became more pronounced. Western Europe became politically and

THE BERLIN WALL

On the morning of August 13, 1961, the citizens of Berlin awoke to find East German soldiers unraveling barbed wire down the middle of the streets that divided the eastern and western sectors. Within a few days, the wire barrier was replaced with a more permanent structure of brick and concrete. When completed, a twelve-foot-high wall wound its way through the center of Berlin and became a grim reminder of the division of Germany into East and West.

The communist government of East Germany built the wall to prevent East Germans from emigrating to the West. For more than twenty-five years, the wall was a symbol of the deep ideological differences that separated democratic and communist governments.

In 1989, the East German government, with approval from the Soviet Union, lifted restrictions on travel to West Germany, thereby eliminating the need for the wall. Germans from both countries celebrated by dancing on the wall and chipping away pieces of it for souvenirs. The destruction of the wall was the first step toward Germany's reunification, which took place in 1990.

economically connected to the United States, and eastern Europe became similarly integrated with the Soviet Union.

BERLIN AND THE DIVISION OF GERMANY

The Soviet government continued to believe Germany was a threat to its national security. Germany and its capital of Berlin had been divided into four sectors after the war, with the Soviet Union controlling the eastern sectors, and the United States, Britain, and France controlling the western sectors. Having been attacked by the Germans in 1914 and again in 1940, the Soviet Union wanted to prevent the restoration of Germany and a resurgence of its military power. In addition, the presence of U.S. troops in West Berlin, located 120 miles inside East Germany, concerned the Soviets. In 1948, the Soviet army blockaded all land transportation into

Berlin. The United States responded by airlifting more than a million tons of food and coal into the city.

For a year, the two superpowers remained at a standstill over Berlin. The blockade ended through negotiations, but Germany and Berlin remained divided. In July 1948, the United States announced the formation of the Federal Republic of Germany. In October, the Soviets declared East Germany to be the new German Democratic Republic. The division of Germany, and of Europe, was complete.

NATO AND THE WARSAW PACT

Fear of the Soviet army in eastern Europe prompted the United States and the nations of western Europe to discuss a regional defense agreement to deter Soviet aggression. In April 1949, they established the North Atlantic Treaty Organization (NATO). Under the terms of the agreement, an attack on one member nation would be considered an attack against all. The initial NATO members were Belgium, Canada, Denmark, France, Great Britain, Iceland, Italy, Luxembourg, the Netherlands, Norway, Portugal, and the United States. In 1952, Greece and Turkey joined; West Germany became the fifteenth member in 1955. Also in 1955, eight eastern European nations—Albania, Bulgaria, Czechoslovakia, East Germany, Hungary, Poland, Romania, and the Soviet Union—formed the Warsaw Pact, a counteralliance to NATO.

3.2 SUPERPOWER COMPETITION

In Europe, the American and Soviet *spheres of influence* were clearly defined: The United States considered the nations of western Europe its allies; the Soviet Union dominated eastern Europe. Elsewhere in the world, however, loyalties were not so clear. As the United States and the Soviet Union competed for power and influence, the East-West conflict spilled into other areas of the world. The Soviets tried to help procommunist groups in Asia and Latin America gain power. American strategists sought to block Soviet moves in these areas, believing in the *domino theory*, which held that if one country became communist, its neighbors would soon "fall" as well.

COMPETITION IN ASIA

China
In the 1940s, China was embroiled in a civil war between the nationalist and communist parties. Supported by the Soviet Union, Chinese communist leader Mao Zedong's forces were able to defeat the U.S.-supported nationalist forces of Chiang Kai-shek in 1949. The fall of a huge country like China to communist rule deeply affected the United States. Americans perceived Mao's victory as an extension of Soviet influence in the Far East, and China's support of communist North Korean forces during the Korean War magnified U.S. apprehension. The fear of further communist expansion in the Far East prompted a change in how the United States viewed Japan. Originally, U.S. officials wanted to prevent Japan from rearming after the war. But now, with Soviet influence spreading, American policymakers began to see the advantages of developing a strong ally in the region. The United States and Japan signed an agreement to station U.S. troops on Japanese soil.

Throughout the 1950s, the Soviet Union sent advisers and financial aid to China, and the two countries formed a powerful communist alliance. But conflicts arose over foreign policy, the location of the Sino (Chinese)-Soviet border, and the best way to implement communism. Relations deteriorated, and in 1960, the Soviets withdrew their advisers and cut off financial and

Cold War tensions between the United States and the Soviet Union were at their peak during the early 1960s. U.S. president John Kennedy and Soviet premier Nikita Khrushchev confronted one another over Berlin, and the Cuban missile crisis in 1962 brought the world perilously close to nuclear war.

In 1972, U.S. president Richard Nixon traveled to China, marking the first diplomatic contact between the two countries in more than twenty years. Here, Nixon meets with Chinese leader Mao Zedong.

technical aid to China. By the late 1960s, relations between the two communist giants approached a warlike state, and China began to look to the United States for a possible alliance.

At the same time, China feared that the United States and the Soviet Union were moving toward friendlier relations. Chinese leaders believed that if the superpowers improved their ties, the United States would be less likely to side with China in the event of a Sino-Soviet war. Chinese leaders acted to head off any possible alliance between the superpowers by seeking friendlier relations with the United States. In 1972, President Richard Nixon visited China. Nixon's visit was the first friendly official contact between the United States and China in more than twenty years. The two countries agreed to increase scientific, cultural, and commercial contacts and open liaison offices in Beijing and Washington to handle business between the two governments. In 1979, President Jimmy Carter established normal relations with China. The two nations exchanged ambassadors, opened trade negotiations, and sought further cooperation in other areas.

Korea

During World War II, Korea was occupied by Japanese troops. In 1945, Soviet leader Joseph Stalin and President Franklin Roosevelt agreed that Japan would surrender to the United States in southern Korea and to the Soviet Union in northern Korea. This temporary division of Korea at the 38th parallel became permanent when the Soviet Union refused to allow the United Nations to supervise national elections in the North. Thus, Korea was divided into two separate countries. Border skirmishes often broke out in the late 1940s between North Korea and South Korea. Finally, in 1950, the Soviets backed a North Korean invasion of South Korea. The United Nations sent troops to repel the invasion, with the United States providing the majority of these forces. Communist China sent soldiers to help North Korea. Although the war ended in a stalemate in 1953, the Korean War demonstrated the United States' determination to fight communist aggression around the world. The Korean War also reversed the United States' post–World War II disarmament efforts, compelling U.S. policymakers to quadruple the defense budget and transform the U.S. military into the most powerful in the world.

Southeast Asia

Like much of Asia, Indochina (Vietnam, Laos, and Cambodia) had been occupied by Japanese forces during World War II. When Japan surrendered, France tried to reassert authority over its three former colonies. In 1946, France granted autonomy to Laos and Cambodia, but the status of Vietnam was problematic. After the Japanese surrender, communist leader Ho Chi Minh proclaimed the independence of Vietnam. When negotiations between Ho and French leaders broke down in 1946, war broke out. After eight years of fierce fighting, the French finally surrendered in 1954. A peace conference established a truce line temporarily dividing Vietnam until nationwide elections could be held.

East Asia was a major battleground of the Cold War. The United States sent troops to Korea in 1950 after communists invaded South Korea. However, the longest Cold War conflict was the Vietnam War. American troops were stationed in Vietnam from 1957 to 1973.

But these elections never took place. Instead, a new political regime proclaimed an independent, U.S.-backed state south of the truce line, while Ho continued to lead a communist government in North Vietnam. Ho Chi Minh accepted aid from the Soviet Union, while the United States agreed to send aid to South Vietnam and to train its army. The United States also sponsored the establishment of the Southeast Asia Treaty Organization (SEATO) to prevent communism from spreading to South Vietnam, Laos, and Cambodia.

In the 1960s and 1970s, the Soviets backed North Vietnam and communist guerrillas in the South in their fight to unify all of Vietnam under communist rule. The United States helped defend South Vietnam with troops and other military aid, eventually spending $146 billion and losing nearly 58,000 American lives. When North Vietnam moved troops into Laos and Cambodia to help in its war effort against South Vietnam, the United States began military efforts in these two countries as well.

By 1968, when Richard Nixon was elected president, Americans were becoming increasingly disillusioned with the war. Peace negotiations led to an agreement in 1973. The agreement called for a cease-fire and the withdrawal of U.S. troops. On March 29, 1973, the last American combat troops left Vietnam, but the Vietnamese armies ignored the cease-fire. In 1975, the communists took over South Vietnam, thereby extending Soviet influence in Southeast Asia. Communist takeovers soon followed in Laos and Cambodia.

COMPETITION IN LATIN AMERICA

Cuba

During the first half of the twentieth century, Cuba—the playground of America's rich—was almost considered a U.S. colony. But most Cubans lived in poverty. The government of pro-American dictator Fulgencio Batista, who ruled from 1952 to 1959, was harsh and corrupt and set the stage for guerrilla leader Fidel Castro's takeover in 1959. Leftists quickly came to dominate Castro's government, instituting a program of sweeping economic and social change. After the United States refused to recognize his new government, Castro turned to the Soviet Union for support. Cuba and the Soviet Union quickly became allies.

In October 1962, the East-West split almost led to nuclear war. The United States discovered that the Soviet Union was secretly constructing launching pads for nuclear missiles in Cuba. For seven days, the world waited as U.S. president John Kennedy and Soviet premier Nikita Khrushchev engaged in tense negotiations. Finally, the Soviets agreed not to station nuclear missiles in Cuba. Many people believed that the world came closer to nuclear war during the Cuban missile crisis than at any other time.

Central America

After Fidel Castro's takeover of Cuba in 1959, the United States began to supply military and economic aid to Central American nations to lessen the likelihood that they too would support communist revolutions or radical political change. In the 1960s, President Kennedy created the Alliance for Progress, an economic aid program that provided funds for roads, schools, hospitals, and water projects. However, in the mid-1970s, the United States stopped aid to some of these countries because President Jimmy Carter believed their governments were engaged in human rights abuses. When Ronald Reagan became president in 1981, he emphasized the U.S. policy of containing the spread of communism throughout the Western Hemisphere. Reagan believed that the United States should strengthen its presence in the region and supply large amounts of economic and military aid to allies in Central America.

In the last years of his presidency, Reagan focused his attention on Nicaragua, where the communist Sandinistas controlled the government and received large amounts of economic and military aid from other communist nations, especially the Soviet Union. Reagan also believed that the Sandinistas were supplying military aid to communist groups fighting in nearby Costa Rica, El Salvador, Guatemala, and Honduras. Cuban and Soviet leaders acknowledged that they were involved in Central America, but only in countries that requested aid or that were fighting for their freedom. Nevertheless, President Reagan convinced Congress of the need to stop communist aggression at America's "back door."

During most of the 1980s, Congress approved millions of dollars in military and economic aid for rebel forces, known as the *contras*, that were fighting the Sandinista government. At the same time, El Salvador also received U.S. economic and military aid to fight communist guerrillas. Using Honduras as a base for the *contras*, the United States built military bases there and established training centers for the Honduran army.

U.S. efforts to curb communist movements in Central America drew criticism from those who charged that the United States was backing military regimes that murdered and tortured their own civilians. However, in Latin America, as in Southeast Asia and other parts of the world during the Cold War, U.S. foreign policy was based on stopping communism even if it meant supporting repressive regimes.

3.3 "THE END OF HISTORY"

During the early 1980s, U.S.-Soviet relations were deteriorating. Both nations continued to escalate the arms race and struggle for control over parts of the world. While the Cold War raged on, however, something was happening on the streets of eastern Europe and the Soviet Union. Decades of oppressive rule and faltering economies were stirring discontent and unrest in the people. Although social and economic problems had been developing for many years in the Soviet Union and eastern Europe, it took a daring new leader, Mikhail Gorbachev, to recognize that reforms had to be made if the Soviet Union and communism were to remain a force in the world.

In 1987, Gorbachev introduced a series of democratic and economic reforms designed to dampen citizen unrest. Few people, including the Soviet leader, expected these reforms to trigger a democratic revolution that would dissolve an empire and alter the global system. The demise of the Soviet Union marked what some called "the end of history," and a new era in international relations was about to begin.

REVOLUTION IN EASTERN EUROPE

The changes Gorbachev introduced to Soviet society triggered a reaction in eastern Europe. Citizens began protesting poor economic conditions and corrupt government officials. To the surprise of some observers in the West, the Soviet Union refrained from sending in troops to stop these revolts as it had done in the past.

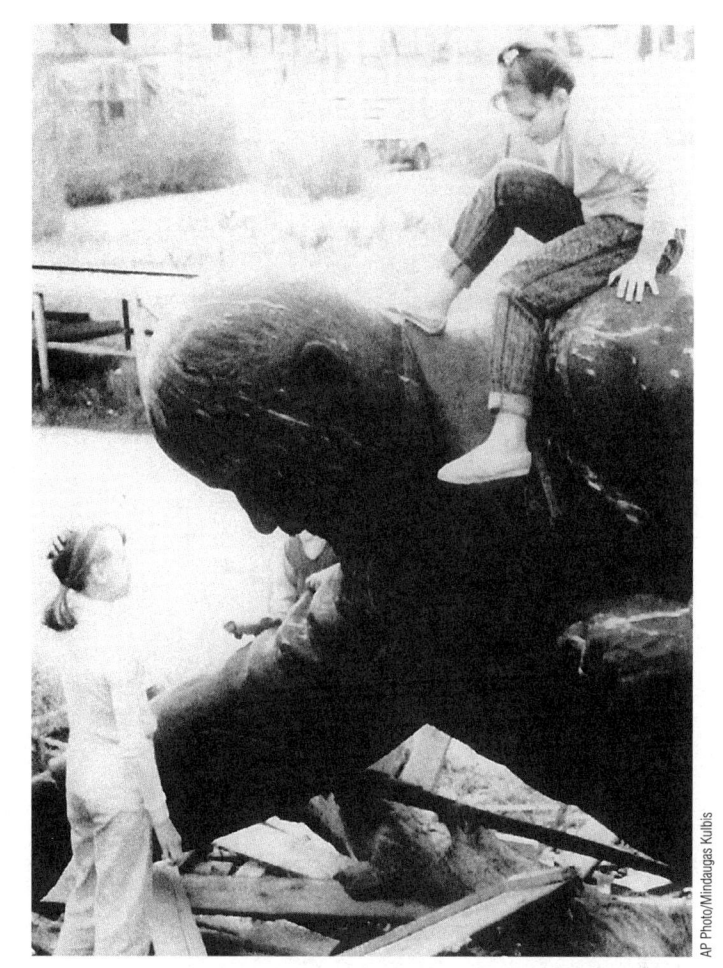

From 1989 to 1991, communism fell throughout eastern Europe, culminating in the collapse of the Soviet Union in December 1991. Here, children play on a toppled statue of Lenin in the former Soviet republic of Lithuania.

THE UNITED STATES AND RUSSIA: AN EVOLVING RELATIONSHIP

In 1983, President Ronald Reagan called the Soviet Union "the evil empire." Seven years later, the Cold War between the United States and the Soviet Union was over. This dramatic transformation in U.S.-Soviet relations began in 1985 when Mikhail Gorbachev became the new Soviet premier. Gorbachev immediately set about improving relations with the United States and began economic and political reform measures, or *perestroika*, in the Soviet Union. He met with President Reagan five times over the next three years, expanding the areas of cooperation between the two countries. In 1987, Reagan and Gorbachev signed the Intermediate-range Nuclear Forces (INF) Treaty, the first agreement to actually eliminate an entire category of weapons in the two nations' nuclear arsenals.

In the late 1980s, U.S.-Soviet relations continued to improve. President George Bush and Gorbachev negotiated new arms-control agreements, and Gorbachev announced that his country would remove its military troops and weaponry from eastern Europe. In 1991, the reforms that Gorbachev himself had introduced in the Soviet Union ultimately caused its collapse and threatened his hold on power. Gorbachev resigned the presidency to Boris Yeltsin on December 25, 1991.

President Vladimir Putin meets with President Bill Clinton in 2000.

When Yeltsin became the president of Russia, he immediately announced a series of democratic and economic reforms. The Clinton administration wholeheartedly supported the Russian president and his reforms. Likewise, Yeltsin cultivated pro-U.S. policies. But Boris Yeltsin's unpredictability and instability eventually eroded his support among Russian citizens and politicians. He resigned in 1999 and appointed Vladimir Putin as his successor. Putin was then elected to his own term in March 2000.

Putin has stated that he will continue the process of democratization and free-market reforms in Russia. However, relations between the new Russian president and the United States government have been tentative so far because of Putin's former involvement in Soviet and Russian intelligence operations, his strict policies toward the breakaway republic of Chechnya, and U.S. fears that he will be too authoritative and undemocratic. As the relationship between Russia and the United States evolves, few doubt the importance of their continued friendship and cooperation in international affairs.

Soviet premier Mikhail Gorbachev meets with President Ronald Reagan and Vice President George Bush in 1988.

The Soviets were allowing their eastern European allies to abandon communism and hold democratic elections. Bulgaria, Czechoslovakia, East Germany, Hungary, Poland, and Romania all held elections in which non-communist parties or newly reformed and renamed communist parties were successful.

Perhaps no nation symbolized the end of the East-West split better than Germany. After more than 200,000 East Germans crossed the newly opened border into West Germany, and thousands more demonstrated for reform at home, East Germany's communist leaders resigned and promised to hold democratic elections. The abandonment of communism in East Germany paved the way for reunification with West Germany. The economies of the two countries were joined in July 1990 when East Germany adopted the West German deutsche mark as its currency. Political union followed on October 3.

THE BREAKUP OF THE SOVIET UNION

As eastern Europe began the transition to democracy and a free-market economic system, and the newly united Germany confronted its own internal challenges, the economic and political stability in the Soviet Union quickly deteriorated.

Seventy years of central control had devastated the Soviet economy. Mikhail Gorbachev's moderate economic reforms did little to dampen the escalating social unrest among the population. In addition, individual Soviet republics began to demand independence from Moscow. First, Latvia, Lithuania, and Estonia broke away despite threats of Soviet military intervention. By early 1991, practically every republic wanted out. Gorbachev tried desperately to hold the union together, but to no avail. On December 25, 1991, Gorbachev resigned. His resignation effectively dissolved the Soviet Union.

Nations watched with amazement, but also with concern. No one was sure how the absence of the Soviet Union and the end of the bipolar balance of power would affect world peace and stability. Suddenly, the longstanding geopolitical structure of the world had vanished. A new era in global relations had arrived. Most people did not know what it would bring.

3.4 A NEW INTERNATIONAL SYSTEM

One of the defining characteristics of the Cold War was *bipolarity*—the division of power between two nations, the United States and the Soviet Union. This global system was in place for more than forty years. Bipolarity evaporated in 1991 before any new structure was ready to replace it, although certain trends have since begun to emerge. The world is now more interdependent and democratic, and free-market economies have been introduced in former communist countries. However, the question over the future balance of power remains.

If global power were determined solely by military strength, then today the world would be dominated by one nation, the United States. No other nation has a military force as powerful as that of the United States. However, according to most experts and leaders, power today is determined more by economic strength.

Although the United States has the strongest economy of any single nation in the world, there are several other nations with large, prosperous economies with which the United States must compete. Therefore, power and influence is likely to be distributed more evenly, making the global system *multipolar*.

But other questions persist. How evenly will power be divided? Will any one nation be the most influential? Will the world's economic powers cooperate with each other in the twenty-first century?

THE BALANCE OF POWER

In many ways, the bipolar system of the Cold War brought a stability to many parts of the world—especially to Europe—that had not been seen in decades. The awesome nuclear arsenals of the United States and Soviet Union were partly responsible for this climate of stability. The threat of nuclear conflict deterred the two superpowers from going to war directly with one another. In addition, the control the two sides had over their respective spheres of influence kept a lid on tensions between smaller nations that might have escalated into war. Although it was dangerous and expensive for both the Soviet Union and United States, the Cold War and bipolarity did create a sense of order. Historian John Lewis Gaddis even called the Cold War "the long peace." Many were afraid that the world might drift into a state of permanent disorder—or even anarchy—in the 1990s. The outbreak of nationalist wars in the former Yugoslavia and blatant aggression like Iraq's invasion of Kuwait made people realize that a world without the Soviet Union would not necessarily be a world without war. The prospect for peace in the future depends mostly on what kind of balance of power is established.

REGIONAL BLOCS

Most experts agree that the new global system is multipolar. History has shown that many poles of power

GLOBAL COMMUNICATIONS AND THE ELECTRONIC REVOLUTION

One of the most important developments affecting how countries relate to one another has been the advancement of information technology. Until fairly recently, rapid, inexpensive communication was possible only between neighboring countries. Today, the Internet, improved telecommunications, and satellite technology have turned the world into what some people are calling a global village.

Mass communication in this new electronic era offers billions of people worldwide the possibility of simultaneously witnessing world events, exchanging important information, and understanding one another better. Technological innovations can also improve the quality of people's lives. For instance, many poor countries do not have the resources to install regular telephone connections in poor or remote villages. In India, employees from a start-up cellular phone company responded to this problem by carrying cell phones to poor villages where few people have telephones in their homes. For a small fee, villagers can use the phones to make their phone calls instead of walking long distances to deliver their messages.

The Internet has opened global communication tremendously. People from around the world can come together in chat rooms to discuss current events and ideas. Family members and friends separated by borders can keep in touch through e-mail for a minimal charge.

Many advocates of the Internet also promote the technology's ability to enhance the process of democratization in the world. They say that repressive dictators cannot isolate their citizens as they could in the past, human rights activists can report abuses in their countries that might have been previously hidden, and citizens in democratic countries can easily communicate their opinions to government officials.

Communication technology also carries risks—such as enabling spies to gather and send sensitive information about military technology across borders or to sabotage companies and governments via computers. Some people also fear that as the global population draws closer together, everyone will be exposed to the same media and Internet culture, and individual cultural differences will erode. Overall, however, world leaders believe that the electronic revolution will foster a greater understanding between nations, improve living standards for individuals, and enable governments to better serve their citizens.

Innovations in communications technology have changed people's lives around the world. Here, a man at the Wailing Wall in Jerusalem holds his cell phone up to allow a relative living in France to say a prayer.

usually lead to a fragmented world, and often to war. Multipolarity existed in the world during the years leading up to World War I and World War II. Because power was dispersed among so many European countries and no alliance to unite them existed, Germany was able to carry out its expansionist policies without retribution until full-scale war broke out.

The sort of multipolarity that existed in the early twentieth century is unlikely to redevelop because economic and military power today is concentrated in only a select group of nations or regions. Competition and conflict in the world in the twenty-first century may therefore be characterized more by competing regions than competing countries.

Some experts and leaders see the world being divided into three regional blocs—North America, Europe, and Asia. Each region has a leader—Japan (and possibly China) in Asia, Germany in Europe, and the United States in North America. There has been a movement over the years by these nations to develop strong ties with their neighbors. The countries of Europe have been working together to create a strong European Union (EU), and many EU economies are already linked by a common currency. The United States, Canada, and Mexico are connected by the North American Free Trade Agreement (NAFTA), which may include other Latin American countries soon. Asia is linked by various economic and security arrangements, although no formal structure exists encompassing all nations in the region.

This move toward greater *regionalization* does not necessarily create tensions and conflict between the different blocs. Although they will compete economically, the United States, Germany, and Japan recognize that cooperation will benefit their economies and their national security. New global agreements are being signed, and old ones are being honored. For example, a revised General Agreement on Tariffs and Trade (GATT) was signed by all trading countries in 1993. In 1995, member nations agreed to extend the Nuclear Non-proliferation Treaty indefinitely.

Cooperation on economic and military issues will continue, many believe, if the leaders of the regional blocs form a coalition based on their shared national interests.

A NEW CONCERT OF POWER?

Is a new "concert of power" emerging? A *concert of power* is a coalition of powerful nations that work together to maintain the balance of power and promote global economic prosperity. However, this sort of global power arrangement has been rare in the past. The most famous coalition was the Concert of Europe in the early nineteenth century—a group of powerful European nations that was able to keep the peace throughout the world by maintaining tight control over other smaller countries. However, the Concert of Europe split apart after only thirty years because of ideological conflicts.

Many see a new concert forming around the United States, the European Union, and the Asia-Pacific region. These countries and regions together could have the necessary military and diplomatic strength to stop military aggression and prevent violations of international law as the United States and Europe proved in 1999, when their governments worked together through NATO to stop Serbian aggression in Kosovo.

For a concert of power to succeed in the long term, its members must be united around a common national interest and be free of ideological disputes. The common interests between the United States, the European Union, and the Asia-Pacific region are economic prosperity and democratic ideology. (Although some Asian countries—particularly China—are not democracies, many have been moving slowly in that direction.)

Experts warn that cultural differences and economic competitiveness could make cooperation between these powers difficult to achieve. However, if world leaders are convinced that working together to maintain global security will improve their own economic and national security, then a concert of power could succeed in keeping the peace and fostering economic growth in the twenty-first century.

THE EMERGENCE OF THE ASIA-PACIFIC REGION

The United States and the European Union, because of their advanced economies, have been centers of power on the international stage for decades. For this reason alone, both will continue to be power centers in the twenty-first century. Nonetheless, they will most likely have to make room for the Asia-Pacific region.

The Asia-Pacific region is the stretch of countries along the Asian side of the Pacific Ocean—an area that begins with China and Japan and ends with Australia and New Zealand. This region of the world received a great amount of global attention during the first half of the 1990s because the combined economic growth rate there was astounding. In 1997, however, many countries in the Asia-Pacific region suffered a devastating economic crisis. Bad loans and investments led to the collapse of currencies in Thailand, Malaysia, Indonesia, and the Philippines. In a domino effect, the economies in neighboring countries, such as South Korea, also took a downturn. The crisis was made even worse by the fact that Japan—the region's economic leader—had been in recession throughout the 1990s. Therefore, despite the Japanese government's efforts to aid other

China's long-term economic growth and possible entry into the World Trade Organization (WTO) have attracted a great deal of investment from foreign corporations such as the U.S. company advertised on this poster in Beijing.

nations in the region, its powers were limited by its own economic problems.

Most economists agree that many of the countries affected by the 1997 crisis have begun to recover. After the International Monetary Fund (IMF) helped Thailand, Indonesia, and South Korea repay their debts, these countries implemented reforms aimed at strengthening their economies and making them less vulnerable to future economic crises. Some other causes for optimism in this region are positive reforms in Japan's economic policies, China's strong economic growth and its possible entrance into the World Trade Organization (WTO), and the lifting of trade barriers between the United States and Vietnam. These factors lead many financial analysts to believe that countries in the Asia-Pacific region should continue to play a leading role in global politics as the twenty-first century progresses.

The Asia-Pacific region and other countries that border the Pacific Ocean—Canada, Chile, Mexico, and the United States—form what is known as the Pacific Rim. Overall, Pacific Rim countries engage in about 50 percent of global trade and worldwide production of goods and services.

The United States and other countries view the Asia-Pacific region as a potentially huge market for their goods and services. Because finding markets in which to sell goods and services is key to a country's economic prosperity, investors around the world will continue to monitor the progress of these countries as they attempt to recover from their economic setbacks.

A Pacific Century?

The Asia-Pacific region's importance to the economic vitality of the United States has led many to believe that it is replacing Europe as the focus of U.S. foreign policy. In 1989, the Asia-Pacific Economic Cooperation (APEC) Forum was formed by nine Asian countries and the United States and Canada to build bridges between nations on both sides of the Pacific Ocean. APEC now has twenty-one members. If economic strength continues to be the dominant factor in determining power in the post–Cold War world, the Pacific Rim could become the most influential component in a new concert of power in the twenty-first century.

Many U.S. policymakers believe that China could eventually equal Japan's influence as an economic leader in the Asia-Pacific region. Economic reforms have allowed the Chinese economy to grow at an annual rate of about 9 percent since the early 1980s, and the country's geographic size and more than 1 billion people give it an advantage in global competition. Therefore, as U.S. policy has increasingly emphasized open trade with Asia in general, in recent years, it has focused on trade relations with China in particular. In the past, the United States based its trade policy toward China on political factors, and many U.S. lawmakers believed that the United States should not give China trading privileges because of its human rights record. However, others said that the potential economic benefits were too great to bypass and that stronger trade relations could open lines of communication that the United States could use to pressure China for political reform.

Following the logic of this last argument, the United States has assisted China in its bid to enter the World Trade Organization, and in 2000, Congress granted China permanent normal trade relations (PNTR).

A WAVE OF DEMOCRACY

In 1950, about twenty-two of the world's countries were considered democracies, representing 31 percent of the world's population. By 2000, 120 countries were electoral democracies with 58 percent of the world's population living in them. What factors contributed to this remarkable trend?

When people living under authoritarian regimes around the world witnessed the destruction of the Berlin Wall and the fall of communist governments across eastern Europe in 1989, many were inspired to start democratic movements in their own countries. Throughout the 1990s, there was an enormous growth in the number of democratic governments installed by elections in which millions of people voted for the first time in their lives. The free-market economic expansion

EUROLAND

On January 1, 1999, the euro became legal tender for Austria, Belgium, Finland, France, Germany, Ireland, Italy, Luxembourg, Holland, Portugal, and Spain. Although no actual euro notes or coins were distributed, the euro can be used for accounting purposes such as personal checks, bank statements, and corporate invoices. These eleven countries—collectively referred to as Euroland—are permanently eliminating their former national currencies and will replace them with freshly printed euros by 2002.

Why is the European Union doing this? Adopting the euro as a common currency is more meaningful than merely changing the pictures on bills and coins. It is actually part of a larger shift in European political cooperation that has taken place over the past fifty years. This cooperation began as a way to ward off the threat of another world war, but as time and the immediate threat of war passed, many European nations began looking for ways to enhance their economic growth, standardize European economic and political policies, and increase trade across European borders.

Supporters of the euro argue that it will eventually have tremendous economic and political benefits through eliminating exchange rates—and the charges that go with them—between participating countries; standardizing European policies by forcing nations to achieve certain economic and political goals before they are granted membership; and giving European countries a unified—and therefore stronger—voice in international politics.

To adopt the euro as its national currency, a country must be a member of the European Union (EU) and meet a set of criteria involving strong economic management. However, some countries that belong to the EU and meet these criteria have decided not to join their neighbors. For example, although Great Britain has traditionally held a position of leadership in Europe, British policymakers remain divided over whether to adopt the euro. Some fear that member countries with weaker economies will slow the strong British economy. Critics of the euro in Great Britain and elsewhere argue that no central European government exists to enforce economic standards, and they point to the euro's poor showing on the foreign exchange market during its introductory year.

Nevertheless, proponents of the new currency say that though it might take time to resolve implementation problems, the euro is here to stay and should eventually be a leading force in a much stronger and more powerful Europe.

One of the most dramatic developments of the post–Cold War world has been the emergence of democracies in eastern Europe, sub-Saharan Africa, and Latin America. Here, voters line up for the 2000 Mexican presidential election, which ended the ruling party's seventy-year grip on power.

in Asia and Latin America created a middle class that felt more empowered to demonstrate against nondemocratic leaders. In addition, the example provided by the United States and democracies in western Europe finally paid off. The combination of these and other factors produced a wave of democracy that swept away authoritarian governments in countries as far apart as Romania, South Africa, and Chile.

The United States, arguing that democracies do not go to war with one another, has always promoted democracy around the world. Many experts maintain that democratic governments are restrained by public opinion and the various checks and balances within their system of government, making it more difficult for a leader to call for military aggression. In addition, democracies are generally viewed as being more committed to finding peaceful resolutions to conflicts. Now that democratic ideals have taken root around the world, the United States and its allies hope that military conflicts will become increasingly rare.

However, many experts warn that this outcome is not inevitable. Although a number of former authoritarian countries have held democratic elections, their leaders do not always stand by democratic principles once they are in office, and they do not take democratization's second, important step—extending civil liberties to their citizens and respecting the rule of law and human rights. For example, since Abdurrahman Wahid was democratically elected president of Indonesia, violent conflict—including fighting between civilians and the Indonesian military—has threatened to tear the nation apart. Vladimir Putin, elected president of Russia in 2000, has used severe military force to put down an independence movement in the Russian republic of Chechnya. And although Alberto Fujimori won the 1990 Peruvian presidential election fairly, many observers say that in the years that followed he became more like a dictator—suspending the constitution, dissolving congress, ignoring presidential term limits, and using the military to retaliate against protesters who said that the 2000 presidential elections, which he won, were not free or fair.

Democratization does not happen overnight, and neither does the peace nor the stability many leaders believe it creates. New democracies may need years to cleanse all traces of authoritarianism from their old political systems and to create appropriate institutions to support the new systems. Once these countries have implemented changes at all levels of society, most experts predict, the longheld belief that more democracy means less war could become a reality.

Overall, the trend toward democracy building continues around the world, and many analysts predict that factors such as increased worldwide access to the Internet will only speed up this process. They believe that if this wave of democracy does continue, ideological conflict—a major cause of the Cold War—will become increasingly rare. With the common interest of economic prosperity and the shared ideology of democracy, world leaders will be more inclined to work together to solve problems. Still, the world faces many challenges that, if not addressed, could derail future attempts at cooperation between nations.

CHAPTER FOUR

WORLD ISSUES TODAY

As international relations undergo fundamental changes, world leaders continue to wrestle with problems of the post–Cold War landscape. Issues such as increasing international trade, military buildups, world development, and environmental degradation are critical concerns. The widening gulf between industrialized and developing countries has made confronting and resolving global problems much more difficult.

Simultaneously, ethnic and nationalist conflicts are erupting in different parts of the world. Ten years after the end of the Cold War, these issues have become more problematic, and perhaps more urgent, than ever before.

4.1 INTERNATIONAL TRADE

People have been exchanging goods for thousands of years. Even when their standard of living was primitive, people still sought spices, textiles, and minerals that could enhance the quality of their lives.

Today, few nations can satisfy all of their people's needs—or desires—with the resources available within their own borders. Thus, international trade allows a nation to obtain goods and services that would not be economical or would be impossible for that nation to produce. World trade is also an important way for a country to increase its supply of money and jobs. Through trade, the economy of a nation grows faster than it would if all goods and services were produced for just its own citizens.

In the past five decades, leaders of the international community have become more aware that the health of one nation's economy can affect the health of other nations' economies. To encourage world trade, leaders meet periodically to discuss economic issues and negotiate agreements on the conduct of trade. They recognize that promoting a stable world economy is in the interest of all nations.

BRETTON WOODS CONFERENCE

Toward the end of World War II, global leaders began to develop the international economic system that exists today. In 1944, leaders of forty-four Western nations met at Bretton Woods, New Hampshire, to create a new monetary system. Under the system developed there,

Some experts say that global trade has become the most important issue in international relations. In recent years, new stock markets have been introduced around the world. Here, a stock trader gestures as he makes a trade at the Singapore International Monetary Exchange.

exchange rates between foreign currencies were fixed against the value of the American dollar. In 1971, the Bretton Woods system was reformed into a *floating exchange system* in which the value of currencies relative to one another are free to change daily. In a floating exchange system, the value of a country's currency generally reflects the health of its economy. Adopting guidelines on currency exchange rates helps to stabilize international trade.

The forty-four countries that participated in the Bretton Woods Conference also agreed to establish the International Monetary Fund (IMF). The major purpose of the IMF is to lend money to nations in need of financial assistance. The IMF had 182 member countries in 2000.

The Bretton Woods Conference proposed the creation of another organization, the World Bank, to assist in financing post–World War II reconstruction projects and to support less-developed nations in their search for credit. Money for loans was to come either from private sources or from the World Bank itself.

GENERAL AGREEMENT ON TARIFFS AND TRADE

In 1947, shortly after establishing the Bretton Woods system, representatives of eighty-three nations signed the General Agreement on Tariffs and Trade (GATT), which established a code of conduct for trading nations. GATT provides an international forum for world leaders to discuss trade issues such as tariffs, quotas, and other forms of protectionism.

GATT negotiations are held periodically to reduce trade barriers worldwide. GATT members—which numbered 134 in 2000—agree that any trade advantage given to one country must be given to all. For example, if the United States reduces a tariff on Australian lamb imports, it must charge other lamb-exporting nations the same lower rate. Traditionally, after GATT negotiation rounds, tariffs drop worldwide because GATT members reduce their tariffs for all other nations.

In 1993, GATT members approved one of the largest trade liberalization treaties in history. The 1993 agreement reduced trade barriers worldwide and created the World Trade Organization (WTO), a body designed to settle trade disputes among member nations.

THE GROUP OF SEVEN

In 1975, leaders of the seven leading noncommunist countries (Canada, France, Great Britain, Italy, Japan, the United States, and West Germany) met for an economic summit to coordinate policies and seek solutions to common problems. The economic summit of the Group of Seven (G-7) nations became an annual event, and in recent years, the group has expanded to allow Russia to play a limited role.

For many years, the leaders of G-7 nations sought to protect their manufacturing industries against increasing foreign competition. At the 2000 G-7 economic summit in Japan, the key issues discussed were the spread of infectious diseases, including AIDS; debt relief for developing countries; improving global financial institutions such as the World Bank; nuclear proliferation; and international action against crime.

REGIONAL TRADE AGREEMENTS

There are exceptions to GATT rules, and some countries use them to negotiate special trade agreements. Such agreements increase trade among the nations involved, although other nations may still face tariffs and quotas. For example, in 1957, nations in western Europe formed the European Economic Community (EC) to improve their economies. By 1992, through a gradual process of eliminating tariffs and quotas, EC members created a single market where money and goods cross borders freely. In 1993, the EC became part of the *European Union* (EU), an economic and security arrangement comprised of fifteen western European nations. The EU may eventually include Turkey and other eastern European nations.

Since the EC was formed, many other countries have also established regional trading blocs. For example, in

Is the Free Market Too Free?

As the forces of globalization bring nations closer together, a country's ability to sell its goods and services on the international market increasingly determines its prosperity. As a result, governments worldwide have been forced to change their policies to survive and succeed in this competitive environment. While some observers believe that globalization could have a number of positive influences on world politics and individual living standards, critics say that it is unfair and destructive to allow impersonal, marketplace forces to decide the future of many of the world's citizens.

Financial institutions such as the International Monetary Fund (IMF) and the World Bank are often targeted by globalization's opponents. Because they require developing countries to carry out certain economic and political reforms before granting them loans, these organizations have a great deal of power to affect governments around the world. Critics of the IMF and the World Bank say those institutions pressure developing countries to adopt policies that ignore the needs of the poor and focus only on improving economic growth. Because these economic reforms create a safer and more profitable environment for foreign investors, opponents say that they actually help foreign corporations much more than the countries where they are implemented.

Critics of globalization argue that a set of environmental and labor standards must be created to regulate multinational corporations—large companies based in more than one country. They say that these corporations often seek out and take advantage of relaxed standards in developing countries to make big profits. Human rights activists contend that many large corporations establish factories in foreign countries where employees must work in poor conditions for long hours with little pay. Environmental activists protest that these large factories do not observe environmental regulations set in their home countries and therefore contribute to global pollution.

Proponents of globalization say that developing countries desperately need the jobs and cashflow that foreign investment brings. They contend that even a low-paying job is better than none and that most multinational corporations pay the same as or more than local companies. They also argue that developing countries cannot afford to institute strict environmental regulations because these kinds of standards would discourage foreign investment. Globalization's supporters believe that economic reforms instituted by developing countries may temporarily place a strain on poorer populations, but in the long run, they will create a more stable economic and political environment that will benefit everyone.

Here, workers sew baseballs at a U.S.-owned factory in Costa Rica.

1993, leaders from the United States, Mexico, and Canada approved the North American Free Trade Agreement (NAFTA), which gradually reduces trade barriers among members and encourages international investment. There are other regional trade blocs, such as the Common Market of the South (Mercosur) in South America and the Association of South East Asian Nations (ASEAN).

Regional trade agreements often help the nations that sign them. They can increase trade, open formerly closed markets, and restrict imports to help struggling industries at home. Although regional trade agreements generally encourage world trade, some leaders believe that they undermine GATT because they give special trade privileges to some nations without lowering trade barriers overall. Some nations, including poorer developing countries, claim that regional trade agreements harm their industries by forcing them to pay higher tariffs than nations that have negotiated special agreements outside GATT.

TRADE AND FOREIGN POLICY

Trade is an essential part of many nations' foreign policy. Countries use trade to promote domestic economic growth, but they can also use trade—or lack of it—as a tool to attain a foreign policy goal. For example, the United States and other nations granted Russia special trading privileges to help convert its economy from communism to capitalism. Sometimes, however, governments use trade to encourage another nation to change its policies. For example, for many years the U.S. government has been concerned that the government of China violates the human rights of its citizens. To encourage Chinese leaders to treat their people more fairly, the United States threatened yearly not to renew China's special trading privilege that reduces tariffs on Chinese imports. However, China's leaders assert that human rights issues are not the concern of foreign nations. Recently, the U.S. Congress passed, and President Clinton signed, a bill granting China permanent normal trade relations. Some members believe that increased trade between the two nations may eventually help bring democratic reform to China.

Through increased international trade, the economies of most nations have become intertwined and mutually dependent. The economic well-being of other countries is within the national interest of most governments. Economic well-being is usually associated with political stability, and a politically stable nation is a more predictable trading partner. Generally, the more nations

Some critics of international institutions such as the World Trade Organization, the World Bank, and the International Monetary Fund say that these organizations too often use their influence to benefit industrialized countries while doing little to alleviate poverty in developing countries.

trade with one another, the greater the chance that they will try to avoid conflicts in other areas.

By the same token, the increased interaction among nations that has accompanied global trade has also raised the potential for conflict. Sometimes trade can lead to disputes among political allies. In 1996, the United States passed the Helms-Burton Act, which allows Americans to sue foreign companies that do business with Cuba. Because many European nations and Canada trade with Cuba, the Helms-Burton Act has strained U.S. relations with those countries. Although these conflicts do arise, nations can cooperate through GATT and through other negotiations to regulate worldwide trade.

4.2 MILITARY BUILDUPS

After World War II, when the United States and the Soviet Union emerged as superpowers, both nations developed new and deadlier weapons, including huge nuclear defense systems. Later, other nations also developed nuclear weapons or the capability to build them. In addition, the superpowers equipped their allies in Europe with both nuclear and conventional (nonnuclear) weapons and sold arms to countries around the world. These sales gave sophisticated, high-tech arms to some nations in conflict with their neighbors. Often these neighbors sought to match the new weapons with arms purchases of their own, fueling a global arms race.

As a result of these military buildups, many countries now own powerful weapons designed not only to defend themselves but also to attack others. The global arms race has fostered conflicts ranging from a civil war in Sudan to intense guerrilla warfare in Colombia. Some of the weapons on these battlefields have come from the United States—ironically, often the first nation called upon to negotiate peace or provide humanitarian relief in war-torn countries.

NUCLEAR PROLIFERATION

Four years after the United States used atomic bombs to hasten the end of World War II in 1945, the Soviet Union developed its own nuclear bomb. However, during the Cold War, the Soviet Union and the United States were not the only nations with nuclear weapons. In 1952, Great Britain exploded its first nuclear device, followed in the early 1960s by France and China. These five countries comprise the "nuclear club." However, other nations now have nuclear capabilities. In 1974, India exploded a nuclear bomb for what it called "peaceful purposes." When India again tested a nuclear bomb in 1998, neighboring Pakistan countered by testing a nuclear device of its own. Experts now estimate that India may have more than seventy nuclear weapons and Pakistan may have almost twenty-five. Some suspect that Israel probably has a nuclear arsenal of around eighty warheads. However, Israeli leaders deny that their country has a nuclear weapons industry.

PROMOTION OF NONPROLIFERATION

For decades, the United States and other nations have tried to limit the spread of nuclear weapons technology. In 1953, the United States designed a program to promote the peaceful uses of nuclear technology in such areas as energy production and medical research. Sponsored through the United Nations, the program, called Atoms for Peace, forbade participating nations from using nuclear technology to make weapons. Although thirty nations agreed to the terms of this program, both France and China independently developed atomic bombs in the 1960s; therefore, Atoms for Peace was judged to be ineffective and was ended.

Another attempt to stop nuclear proliferation was the Treaty of Tlatelolco in 1967. The purpose of the treaty

Shown here, a long-range, nuclear-capable missile is displayed during the January 1999 Republic Day Parade in New Delhi, India. Some experts believe that nuclear proliferation in developing countries will be the greatest threat to global security in the twenty-first century.

was to make Latin America a "nuclear-free zone." Individual Latin American countries agreed not to test, manufacture, or acquire nuclear weapons. In the 1980s, this treaty proved ineffective as Brazil and Argentina pursued nuclear weapons programs. However, both countries have since renounced their programs, ratified the Treaty of Tlatelolco, and agreed to allow inspections of their nuclear energy facilities.

In 1968, a worldwide nuclear nonproliferation treaty was signed. The General Assembly of the United Nations approved the Nuclear Nonproliferation Treaty (NPT), which was intended to halt the spread of nuclear weapons and promote peaceful uses of nuclear power. As of early 2000, 187 countries had signed the NPT. Cuba, India, Israel, and Pakistan were the only ones that had not. However, signing the treaty does not necessarily mean that a nation's leaders will abide by its provisions. Several signatories, including Algeria, Iran, Iraq, Libya, and North Korea, are suspected of trying to develop nuclear weapons.

When the NPT came up for renewal in 1995, delegates voted to extend the treaty indefinitely. Representatives also agreed to annually review nuclear disarmament efforts by the nuclear club.

Despite these efforts by the international community to stop the spread of nuclear weapons, experts believe that a number of nations have the capability to develop and deliver a nuclear bomb. As more countries possess nuclear arms, the danger that these powerful weapons will be used may increase. World leaders believe that developing sound global treaties and accurate methods of verifying compliance is key to the security of all nations.

ARMS REDUCTION

As nations around the world have worked to prevent the spread of nuclear weapons, the United States and the Soviet Union—now Russia—have worked together to limit and reduce their existing stockpile of nuclear warheads. The two countries took the first steps during the Cold War. In 1969, the Soviet Union and the United States opened the Strategic Arms Limitation Talks (SALT I). These eventually led to the 1972 signing of the Anti-Ballistic Missile (ABM) Treaty, which limited strategic missile defense systems, and the Interim Agreement, which limited some offensive weapons. In 1979, the SALT II Treaty was signed, further limiting arms production.

In 1982, arms control took a new turn when the two superpowers began negotiating the reduction of their existing nuclear weapons at the Strategic Arms Reduction Talks (START I). The START I Treaty was signed in 1991, and a START II Treaty—further reducing nuclear weapons—was finally ratified by the lower house of the

Russian parliament in April 2000. The START II Treaty calls for the United States and Russia to gradually reduce their nuclear stockpiles. At the time of START II ratification, Russia had 6,472 warheads while the United States had 7,763. The United States and Russia hope to continue arms reductions by negotiating a START III agreement in the near future.

ANOTHER ARMS RACE?

For many years, the United States has discussed the possibility of a nuclear missile defense system to protect the country from an incoming nuclear attack. The idea began as the "Star Wars" program under President Ronald Reagan. However, at that time, the cost of building such a system was astronomical, and many believed it would not work. Thus, the program was put aside. However, some believe new technology has made possible the development of a less-expensive missile defense system. As more countries around the world become capable of making and delivering their own nuclear weapons, the idea of a nuclear defense system has gained popularity in the United States. Supporters say that the threat of accidental launch or nuclear attack will only increase in the future, and the United States must act to offset this threat.

Although criticism is strong, the United States has begun testing missiles for the missile defense program. Opponents say that it violates the ABM Treaty signed by the United States and Russia in 1972. They argue that this treaty is the basis of later U.S.-Russian arms reduction treaties such as START I and II, and if one treaty is violated, the others will be meaningless. Such critics also point to numerous failed tests as evidence that a working, cost-effective system cannot be currently developed. Opponents in Russia and China say that a missile defense system would give the United States an unfair and dangerous advantage, allowing U.S. leaders to fearlessly disregard international law. Some even say that the creation of the system could trigger another arms race. U.S. supporters of the defense system have attempted to negotiate a broader ABM Treaty with Russia and to reassure China and Russia that the system would only protect the United States from countries with a small number of nuclear weapons.

According to the Strategic Arms Reduction Talks II (START II), the United States and Russia will gradually reduce their nuclear stockpiles. However, as the United States and Russia dismantle these weapons, the risk increases that some of this nuclear material will be illegally sold or traded. Thus, the dismantling and storage (shown above) of nuclear weapons must be carefully monitored.

ARMS SALES

While even one nuclear weapon in a region can be disruptive to its balance of power, large numbers of conventional weapons can be equally destabilizing. During the Cold War, the United States and the Soviet Union sold their allies conventional weapons, such as tanks and high-tech missiles. Most of these weapons went to industrialized countries, usually those in NATO or the Warsaw Pact. But in the late 1960s, both superpowers began to send more weapons to developing countries. The superpowers used arms sales to compete for allies among less-developed states, replace humanitarian aid, and transfer technology to friendly nations. Many weapons went to the volatile Middle East. Later, arms sales were made to countries in Africa and Latin America. Other major weapons producers, including China, France, and Great Britain, also sell weapons to other nations. The result is that more nations today own sophisticated fighter aircraft, tanks, guns, and missiles that are capable of carrying nuclear or chemical weapons—weapons that are largely uncontrolled by international agreements. Some policymakers fear that this high volume of worldwide weapons sales means a greater risk of war.

Some arms purchasers are involved in regional conflicts. Yet, without the continual supply of weapons, they would have lost the means to fight years ago. For example, Sudan's civil war between its Islamic fundamentalist government and its non-Muslim population has been fueled in part by other countries. The Sudanese government reportedly receives support from Iran and Saudi Arabia, while the non-Muslims allegedly receive military aid from Uganda, a neighboring Christian nation that does not want a fundamentalist Islamic country on its border. Without the supply of foreign weapons and money, the warring parties in Sudan might have been forced to reach a peace settlement long ago.

At the end of the Cold War, the Soviet Union was the world's largest exporter of conventional arms, responsible for 32 percent of all world arms transfers in 1989. However, since the dissolution of the Soviet empire, Russia's share in world arms transfers fell to 15 percent in 1999. Although overall arms purchases have decreased somewhat in the post–Cold War era, the U.S. share of world arms sales grew to about 50 percent in 1999. Most U.S. arms sales go to Egypt, Israel, Saudi Arabia, Singapore, and Taiwan.

Arms sales allow weapons-producing countries to make money and to sell equipment no longer needed at home. Sales also help to generate goodwill with the purchasing nations. However, some fear these weapons may lead their purchasers to fight wars instead of seeking other ways to solve problems.

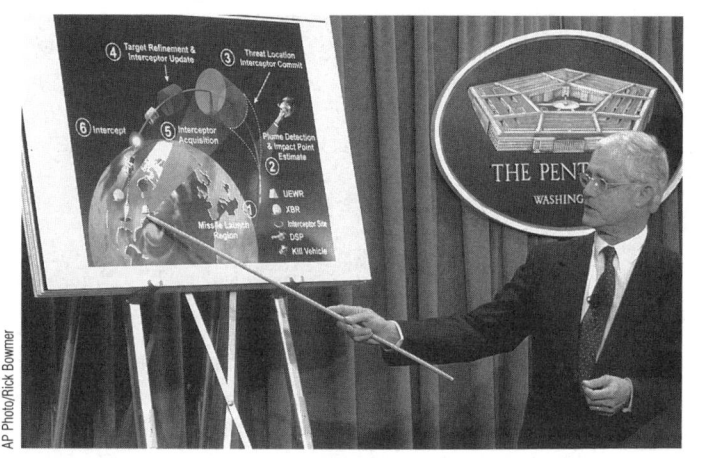

To protect Americans from a possible nuclear attack, the U.S. government has begun developing a nuclear missile defense system. Here, a Pentagon official explains the proposed system to reporters in June 2000.

4.3 NATIONALISM AND ETHNIC CONFLICT

The end of the Cold War unleashed a fierce tide of ethnic, tribal, and religious conflicts in many parts of the world. Between 1989 and 1999, 97 out of 103 global armed conflicts were internal. These conflicts are especially pronounced in areas once ruled and influenced by the former Soviet Union, most notably eastern Europe. For example, internal conflict has persisted in the former Yugoslavia since 1991. There are more than 100 ethnic or minority disputes in the former Soviet Union alone. Similar disputes exist in countries as far apart as Canada, Indonesia, and Sudan.

Often the sides in these clashes are driven by the forces of *nationalism*. A state or country—a centralized political system, with recognized borders and a territory, that governs the population therein—is commonly called a *nation*. Nationalism comes from a lesser-used definition of nation—a community of people who see themselves as a distinct group on the basis of common ancestry, history, society, institutions, ideology, language, territory, and sometimes religion. People of one nation distinguish themselves from people of other nations and countries. Nationalism refers to one nation or a group's promotion of its culture and interests above those of other nations or groups.

By recent accounts, there are more than 3,500 groups of people in the world that consider themselves "nations," but there are fewer than 200 officially recognized states. As more and more groups fan nationalist flames and vie for political power or independence, the potential for increasing violent conflicts worldwide is alarming. In the former Yugoslavia and other places with ethnic conflicts, nationalism has taken on sinister qualities. Combatants view each other not as fellow citizens, but as members of enemy ethnic groups. The resulting hatred enables them to commit grave atrocities against people with whom they once lived peacefully. Perhaps this surge in nationalism and ethnic conflict explains why more than 90 percent of all war casualties during the 1990s were civilians.

Why have nationalism and ethnic conflicts reemerged in the post–Cold War world? During the Cold War, the superpower rivalry between the Soviet Union and the United States stifled ethnic and religious conflicts within the countries they influenced. But after the Soviet Union broke up, various ethnic groups, many in eastern Europe or the former Soviet republics, reemerged to claim power.

Nationalist struggles often result in civil wars and in the breakup of countries. These conflicts can produce floods of refugees and terrible human suffering. Many believe that the international community needs to find effective ways to address these conflicts.

SPLINTERING EFFECTS OF SEPARATISM

Separatism is a form of nationalism. A separatist movement emerges when a group within an already-recognized state wants to form its own country. Such groups base their claim on the right of self-determination, or the belief that a group of people should be able to create their own form of government, separate from outside control or influence.

Yugoslavia's Nightmare

During the Cold War, Yugoslavia was a united country composed of many ethnic groups, divided by religion. The majority of Yugoslavs belonged to one of three groups—Croats (mostly Roman Catholics), Serbs (mostly Orthodox Christians), and Muslims. These populations were mixed throughout each of Yugoslavia's five republics and kept in line by a central communist government influenced by the Soviet Union. The Soviet empire and the Yugoslav federation suppressed conflict among Yugoslavia's diverse population with powerful, centralized governments and strong armies. However, when the Soviet Union began to break apart in 1990, Yugoslavia's long-simmering ethnic hatreds tore the country apart. The dominant republic of Serbia wanted to maintain its power over the other Yugoslav republics, while some of the other republics wanted independence. In 1991, the republics of Slovenia and Croatia fought against Serbia and won independence.

However, the independence movement did not go as smoothly in the republic of Bosnia-Herzegovina. When Bosnia declared its independence from Yugoslavia in October 1991, its population was 44 percent Muslim, 31 percent Serb, and 16 percent Croat. The Serbs living in Bosnia feared that the Muslim-dominated Bosnian government would create a Muslim state, and Serbs wanted to live separate from the Croats, their enemies since World War II. Therefore, the Bosnian Serbs declared war against Muslims and Croats, with the goal of creating their own country within Bosnia. The brutal Serbian policy of "ethnic cleansing"—the killing or displacing of people based on their ethnic origin—was

After NATO forced Serbian troops out of Kosovo in 1999, conflict continued between ethnic Albanians and Serbs living in Kosovo. NATO peacekeepers remained in Kosovo to restore peace and stability, but at times they have become involved in clashes between the groups. Here, ethnic Albanians throw stones at peacekeepers.

an attempt to make the Bosnian part of "Greater Serbia" ethnically pure. After witnessing both sides of the Bosnian conflict commit violent atrocities, European and world leaders stepped in to try to resolve the conflict. In 1995, the United States negotiated the Dayton Accords, a peace treaty that divided Bosnia into a Muslim-Croat federation and a Serb republic.

Violence in the former Yugoslavia continued in the Serbian province of Kosovo. Kosovo was ruled largely by ethnic Albanians until 1989, when Yugoslav president Slobodan Milosevic rose to power and installed Serbian police rule. Ethnic Albanians responded by creating the Kosovo Liberation Army (KLA) to fight for the province's independence.

In the spring of 1998, Serbian special forces began to crack down on the KLA, and in March 1999, Milosevic sent troops into Kosovo. These troops, along with Serbians living in Kosovo, forced tens of thousands of ethnic Albanians to leave. Shocked by the atrocities and human misery, the United States and other NATO forces began a bombing campaign that forced Milosevic to withdraw his troops about three months later. With the help of NATO troops, Albanian refugees returned to their homes. However, violence continued in the province because ethnic Albanians began retaliating against Serbian civilians living in Kosovo.

When the people of Serbia forced Slobodan Milosevic to cede his presidency to fairly elected Vojislav Kostunica in October 2000, the leaders of Europe were hopeful that Kostunica would usher in a new era of peace. Otherwise, these leaders feared, Yugoslavia's violence and disorder would spread across Europe, jeopardizing more than thirty-five years of work toward European unity.

UNITED NATIONS PEACEKEEPING

When conflicts cause large-scale humanitarian crises, outside countries sometimes believe they are morally obligated to intervene, usually under the flag of the United Nations (UN). Member countries around the world send money, troops, and weapons to support UN peacekeeping interventions. Recently, UN peacekeepers have carried out a broad variety of missions in locations from Kosovo to Sierra Leone. Their duties included distributing food supplies to famine victims, building temporary housing for refugees, enforcing peace agreements, promoting democratization, and disarming rebel groups.

Although these missions were at least partly successful, critics believe that the United Nations has overcommitted itself to action in numerous conflicts around the world. They argue that some multilateral UN missions have suffered from ill-defined goals and objectives and insufficient organization and financial backing. Many Americans question whether humanitarian and peacekeeping operations are worth endangering American lives and spending billions of taxpayer dollars. Opponents of these missions also believe that engaging in many of these conflicts is not in the U.S. national interest. Citizens of other countries where troops have been committed to UN peacekeeping missions share similar concerns. Some experts say that this lack of commitment has resulted in UN-member countries not sending enough money, troops, or equipment to make peacekeeping missions successful. In conflicts in Afghanistan, the Basque region of Spain, Northern Ireland, and Sri Lanka, most world leaders and UN officials have chosen not to become involved.

Many experts believe that it is now crucial that world leaders work together to decide their criteria and goals for intervention.

Turmoil after the Empire

The former Soviet Union's powerful central government once ruled peoples of many ethnic and religious backgrounds. However, with the dissolution of the Soviet empire in 1991, nationalist movements emerged. Chechnya, a primarily Muslim republic of Russia, declared independence from Russia in 1991. Chechnya is a strategically located, oil-rich territory in the region of the Caucasus Mountains on Russia's southern flank. Russian president Boris Yeltsin insisted it was still part of Russia and sent 40,000 troops to Chechnya in December 1994 to force its submission to Moscow. By May 1995, virtually all of Chechnya was once again under Russian control, and the Russian military continued to occupy Chechnya. However, conflict between Chechnya and Russia continued. More fighting in 1996 ended in a cease-fire agreement in which Russia agreed to withdraw its troops from Chechnya. This led Chechnya to become more independent of Russia. Chechens installed courts and legal institutions that followed Islamic law, elected a Chechen president, and built a new national guard to protect Chechnya from Russian invasion. Russia did not interfere with these procedures until Chechen terrorist acts against Russian civilians increased sharply and Chechen Islamic militants invaded the neighboring Russian republic of Dagestan in 1999. This time, Russia, under Yeltsin and his newly appointed prime minister, Vladimir Putin, reacted by heavily bombing Chechen cities and farmland. This "scorched earth" policy reduced the capital city, Grozny, to rubble and left the Chechen economy in ruins. Likewise, the economic costs for Russia's military action were enormous. Although the Russian campaign significantly weakened the Chechen independence movement, terrorist attacks against Russian civilians have continued, and observers say that the conflict is not over.

"Velvet" Separatism

Although violent separatist movements receive more of the world's attention, countries can split apart without bloodshed. In 1989, communist rule in Czechoslovakia fell to a peaceful democratic movement called the "Velvet Revolution." The population of Czechoslovakia was mostly comprised of two ethnic groups: Czechs of Austrian and German heritage and Slovaks of Hungarian descent. However, when establishing their new government, the people of Czechoslovakia could not agree on which group should hold power. Therefore, in January 1993, Czechoslovakia peacefully split into two countries—the Czech Republic and Slovakia—so that each nation could govern itself.

The Basques are an ethnic group that lives in the western Pyrenees of France and Spain and desires to create a separate Basque nation, apart from French and Spanish control. Here, supporters of the Basque nationalist party, Herri Batasuna, march in northern Spain in 1999. Some Basque separatists use terrorism to advance their cause.

Separatism also exists in North America. Many people in Canada's province of Quebec have peacefully pushed for self-determination since the 1960s. Quebec's French-speaking population fears losing its cultural identity to Canada's English-speaking majority. Canada's leaders have resisted granting independence to Quebec because they fear other groups, particularly American Indian tribes, may also demand independence. Furthermore, they believe that Quebec's secession would damage Canada's economy and the North American Free Trade Agreement.

STRUGGLES FOR POWER

Sometimes nationalist groups resort to war because a particular side (or sides) wishes to control the existing government or state but does not necessarily want to carve up the country. In sub-Saharan Africa, such nationalist movements often break down along tribal lines. Other nationalist conflicts arise out of religious tensions. Many religious conflicts involving fundamentalist Islam have erupted in areas such as Central Asia and North Africa.

Islamic Fundamentalism
Islam is an all-encompassing faith; its culture governs not only individual behavior and ethics but also societal organization and governmental policies. Therefore, Islam in its most conservative form, called Islamic fundamentalism, is a way of life for its followers. Countries that are run by fundamentalist Islamic governments (including Afghanistan, Iran, and Sudan) provide stark contrasts to Western-style democracies in which church and state are usually separate. These differences in philosophies often cause nationalist conflicts in countries where Muslim and Western influences overlap or meet.

For example, in 1992, the government of Algeria—a former French colony in northern Africa—decided to cancel a second round of parliamentary elections when it appeared that an Islamic party would win. Islamic fundamentalists then declared a "holy war" on the Algerian government, seeking to install their own Islamic state. When the Islamic party failed to win the 1995 presidential elections, its members began to massacre large numbers of civilians. A new president, Abdelaziz Bouteflika, was elected in 1999 and began an offensive against Islamic guerrillas in a bid to end the civil war. The offensive was successful for a time, but in July 2000, 1,200 civilians were massacred by the guerrillas. The estimated death toll of Algeria's civil war now exceeds 100,000.

Islamic fundamentalist movements also emerged in the former Soviet republics in Central Asia. When the Soviets took over these areas in the early twentieth century, they repressed the Muslim practices of people in this primarily Islamic region. Today, in some Central Asian countries there are tensions between Russian-influenced governments and Islamic movements.

Ethnic Conflict in Africa
In sub-Saharan Africa, some recent civil wars have been fought along ethnic lines. For example, since 1993, interethnic violence has killed more than 150,000 people in the small African country of Burundi. The Tutsis and Hutus there are divided by both tribal and class lines. In the past, members of the Tutsi governing class initiated violence in Burundi to maintain their status through brutal military control. Today, an armed movement led by Hutus from the Burundi countryside has challenged the government. Both sides have committed atrocities and participated in ethnic cleansing in their fight for power.

Emergency humanitarian aid to refugees of Rwanda's civil war in 1994 probably saved the lives of more than 100,000 people in camps like the one shown here. However, the end of Rwanda's ethnic war has not brought an end to hostilities between members of the Hutu and Tutsi tribes.

In 1994, a brutal civil war between Hutus and Tutsis erupted in the neighboring country of Rwanda. The Hutu militia tried to commit genocide against the minority Tutsi population, resulting in the deaths of almost 800,000 Tutsis in three months. Tutsis responded by driving the Hutu government and army into neighboring Zaire, which is now called the Democratic Republic of the Congo. Ethnic conflict between Rwandan Hutus and Tutsis persists and has spread to the Congo.

The tragedies in Rwanda and Burundi illustrate the most violent and shameful face of nationalism. As similar disasters continue to unfold and require outside intervention, world leaders are beginning to stress the value of human rights and international stability over national self-determination. Moreover, as separatist movements threaten to splinter existing states and ignite nationalism in other countries, world leaders must learn to help resolve ethnic and nationalist conflicts quickly and fairly. Otherwise, continuing hatred and prolonged civil wars could spill over into nearby countries, just as the Rwandan conflict has spread to the Congo. When countries become embroiled in ethnic conflicts, their governments flounder or become nonexistent. Nationalist disorder makes it difficult for world leaders to cooperate on other important issues such as security and trade. Therefore, uncontrolled ethnic and nationalist movements threaten international stability.

4.4 THE DEVELOPING WORLD

The United Nations Development Program defines development as "a process of enlarging people's choices." According to the UN, the most critical choices are to lead a long and healthy life, to be educated, and to have access to resources needed for a decent standard of living. Additional choices include political freedom, guaranteed human rights, and self-respect. Achieving these goals universally has proven elusive, however, as drought, war, hunger, and disease continue to stymie global efforts to improve living standards. Yet experts warn that without new solutions, problems in the developing world could worsen, particularly if population growth there is not curtailed.

THE NORTH-SOUTH GAP

Throughout the eighteenth and early-nineteenth centuries, countries in the Northern and Southern Hemispheres took divergent economic paths. In general, the nations of northern Europe and North America began to industrialize, building strong economies and strong global leadership. Meanwhile, the people of the arid or tropical nations in the Southern Hemisphere and some tropical countries in the Northern Hemisphere remained primarily dependent on agriculture, although their climates and soil did not always produce enough food or textiles for their needs. Over time, the economic differences between the nations of the North and South became more pronounced, resulting in a phenomenon called the *North-South gap*: the North has become increasingly wealthy while the South has largely remained mired in poverty.

The South has not developed in part because of the traditional pattern of world trade. Historically, the South has exported raw materials and cash crops to the North, and the North in turn has exported manufactured products and technology to the South. This

The U.S. Peace Corps sends Americans overseas to initiate projects to help developing countries to become more self-sufficient. Shown here, a Peace Corps volunteer helps a local fish farmer in Nepal.

WORLD ISSUES TODAY 77

WORLD POPULATION (BILLIONS) 1950–2050

While UN statistics show that population figures for more-developed regions have remained about the same since 1950, the population in less-developed countries has almost tripled. If UN estimates are accurate, by 2025, people in less-developed countries will outnumber those in more-developed countries by more than 5 to 1. This projection indicates there may be great demands on world resources such as food, water, and energy in the next century.

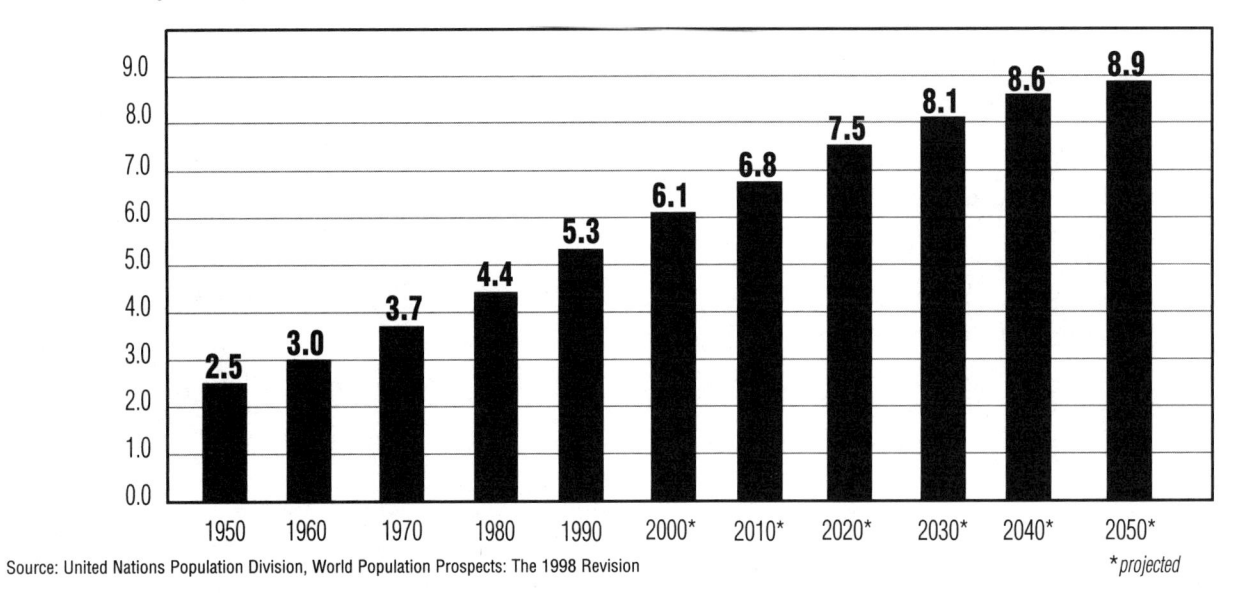

Year	Population (billions)
1950	2.5
1960	3.0
1970	3.7
1980	4.4
1990	5.3
2000*	6.1
2010*	6.8
2020*	7.5
2030*	8.1
2040*	8.6
2050*	8.9

Source: United Nations Population Division, World Population Prospects: The 1998 Revision
*projected

pattern has favored the North because, in general, the prices of raw materials and food have increased more slowly than those of manufactured products and technology have.

The developing world's concerns, including freshwater resources, housing, and poverty, are different from those of industrialized nations. However, providers of humanitarian aid and multilateral organizations—most notably the United Nations—are helping to give voice to the problems of the developing world. The continuing battle, however, lies in gaining the attention of those nations best poised to help—the industrialized nations. Ironically, the North once had great interest in the developing world, but they did so as colonial powers rather than as benefactors.

SELF-DETERMINATION IN THE POSTWAR ERA

Prior to World War II, most of the developing world was controlled by European colonial powers, including France, Great Britain, the Netherlands, Portugal, and Spain. In

1945, only four African nations were independent—Egypt, Ethiopia, Liberia, and South Africa. The rest of Africa was ruled by foreign powers. Much of Asia—including Burma, Ceylon, India, and Nepal—was ruled by Britain. Great Britain, France, and the Netherlands maintained colonies in Asia, South America, and the Caribbean.

However, new thinking challenged colonialism during World War II. In 1941, when British prime minister Winston Churchill and U.S. president Franklin Roosevelt met to discuss war strategy, the two leaders also produced a plan to keep peace once the war was over. In a document that came to be known as the Atlantic Charter, Churchill and Roosevelt criticized colonization by many European powers. They also affirmed the right of *self-determination,* or the right of all people to choose their own form of government. The concept of self-determination became a guiding force in the postwar era.

With the creation of the United Nations in 1945, the movement toward liberation from colonial powers began. A special office of the United Nations, the Trusteeship Council, was created to assist colonies in their transition from colony to independent nation. From 1945 to 1994, more than seventy-five nations became independent. The Trusteeship Council suspended operation in November 1994, after Palau—the last remaining United Nations trust territory—attained independence.

But independence rarely solved the problems of the former colonies. In many of the new nations, people did not necessarily share a common history, common culture, or common language. Colonial powers had determined their borders, often mixing peoples of different backgrounds and beliefs. Many times, civil wars erupted when factions vied for control within these artificial boundaries.

According to the United Nations Development Fund, 1.2 billion people worldwide survive on less than one dollar a day. Although the percentage of poverty-stricken people is expected to drop in coming years, population growth will cause the actual number of poor people to rise. Shown here, an Egyptian girl walks through her neighborhood in Cairo.

The United States and the Soviet Union saw in these new nations an opportunity to extend their influence. Many of the nations controlled strategic minerals or vital resources. The superpowers became involved in civil wars in newly independent nations, including Korea, Vietnam, Angola, and Nicaragua. The Soviet Union aided communist factions, while the United States aided anticommunist factions. However, as the Cold War began to thaw in the 1980s, the superpowers generally withdrew from military conflicts in developing countries.

POVERTY IN DEVELOPING COUNTRIES

More than 1 billion people live in conditions unimaginable to most Americans. In developing countries, food and water are scarce, and health standards are low—leading to high rates of infant mortality, shorter life spans, and rampant disease. Often more than 50 percent of the population cannot read or write. Few villages have plumbing, electricity, or paved roads. People still farm with the most basic tools and techniques, and there is little industry. In most countries, land and income are unequally distributed. Average incomes in the least-developed countries are sometimes less than $400 per year, although a tiny percentage of the population enjoys considerable wealth.

Many poor people are also hungry. Despite advances in agricultural technology and years of international aid programs, large numbers of starving and malnourished people still exist. According to the Worldwatch Institute, about 1.2 billion people in developing countries suffer from *undernourishment* (a lack of protein and calories) or *malnutrition* (a lack of proper nutrients).

In less-developed countries, hunger is the result of droughts, civil wars, famines, and population growth. At the end of the 1990s, the largest number of hungry people lived in India and Bangladesh. However, the worst starvation has occurred in sub-Saharan Africa, where the number of people suffering from hunger presently includes almost one-third of the region's total population. This problem can be partially attributed to decreased regional food production throughout the 1980s accompanied by population growth. In addition, civil wars often disrupt the food supply and distribution networks, resulting in food shortages or famines. Recurring drought and other natural disasters also contribute to starvation in sub-Saharan Africa.

Population growth is a fundamental problem in developing countries. For example, women in western Africa average 6.2 births in their lifetime. The high birth rates in many of these areas overburden already weak systems of food supply, medical care, education, and other basic social services. Furthermore, population experts predict that almost all global population growth between now and 2050 will occur in developing countries—a trend that points to more famine and humanitarian crises in these regions.

FOREIGN AID

Each year the industrialized nations send billions of dollars to help developing countries. In 1999, official international development assistance to developing countries

As many countries decrease their foreign-aid spending, nongovernmental organizations, such as Medecins Sans Frontiers (Doctors Without Borders) and the International Committee for the Red Cross, have had to take on additional development duties.

THE EFFECT OF AIDS ON DEVELOPMENT

In human terms alone, the devastation that AIDS is causing in many African countries is hard to imagine. The Worldwatch Institute reports that some southern African countries could lose up to one-third of their populations to the disease over the next ten years and that the number of orphans could reach 20 million by 2010.

The effect of AIDS on development in sub-Saharan Africa may be just as devastating. For instance, food production may drop off dramatically if farmers contract AIDS or have to care for loved ones with the disease. The same problem applies to other industries. When employers must constantly hire and train new workers to replace those who have died of AIDS, production declines and becomes more expensive. In turn, economic growth slows down or even stops.

Education is one of the few areas where many African countries have made improvements in recent decades. It is unfortunate, however, that AIDS is reversing some of that progress. In Zambia, for example, the number of teachers dying of AIDS each year is close to the number of new teachers in training, and in the Central African Republic, more than 100 primary schools have had to close because of a shortage of teachers.

AIDS will also have a tremendous impact on health care. In Zimbabwe, nearly half of the health care budget is spent on treating AIDS patients. An industrialized country might be able to cover this cost, but the majority of developing countries already struggle to provide their citizens with adequate health care. Less money for doctors and medicine generally means that the AIDS epidemic will even affect the health of people who do not have the disease.

The millions of children who are orphaned by AIDS will affect the future of sub-Saharan countries. AIDS orphans often turn to crime, drugs, or prostitution to survive, continuing the cycle of HIV infections and increasing crime rates.

Poverty, hunger, lack of education, and crime are all destabilizing factors, leading some observers to believe that the AIDS epidemic could increase political instability in countries facing this crisis. They say it is imperative that industrialized countries increase foreign assistance for AIDS-related projects to prevent future infections, to care for AIDS patients and orphans, and to counteract the economic and developmental destruction that the disease is causing. Otherwise, these observers fear that AIDS will reverse much of the development that African countries have achieved so far.

---

totaled $27.9 billion. This aid provides food for the hungry, medicine for the sick, and education for the young. Foreign aid also helps developing countries defend themselves. Military aid helps such nations buy weapons, train soldiers, and build factories so they can manufacture their own military supplies.

Industrialized countries historically have given aid to developing countries that are strategically important or have similar ideologies. Today, the United States and Japan are the two largest donors of foreign aid. However, the U.S. government spends less on foreign aid today, as a percentage of the federal budget, than it did during the Cold War. For example, in 1949, foreign aid consumed 21 percent of the budget; in 2000, it accounted for less than 1 percent of all federal spending. In 2000, the United States spent about $22.4 billion in foreign aid. Only about 40 percent of this money will go for economic, humanitarian, and development assistance to less-developed countries. The U.S. share of world assistance has dropped from 63 percent in the 1950s to less than 15 percent in 1997. France and Germany also donate large sums to developing countries. Sweden,

Norway, and Denmark spend the highest percentage of their gross domestic product (GDP) on foreign aid.

Other kinds of foreign assistance take the form of loans. However, many developing nations have taken out more loans than they can afford to repay. Some countries pay more per person on servicing foreign debts than on health and education. Thus, while loans were supposed to help their economies grow, excessive loans have actually worsened the standard of living in many less-developed nations.

Clearly, the countries of the developing world face many problems. They are plagued by famine, disease, continuing poverty, increasing population, and growing debt. In a world where the economies of all nations are increasingly intertwined, industrial countries could be affected by the economic health of developing nations. Likewise, the fate of many of the less-developed nations will most likely depend on the economic policies made by the United States and other developed countries.

4.5 THE ENVIRONMENT

Environmental problems in one country, such as acid rain and deforestation, can affect many other countries. Thus, the environment has become a global issue, requiring international cooperation. However, most solutions to environmental problems involve tremendous cost to the polluting nation's businesses or consumers. Most governments are unwilling to make their people pay for environmental cleanups if other nations are not making similar sacrifices. These governments fear that creating laws forcing domestic businesses to adopt expensive, environmentally friendly practices will reduce their ability to compete with unrestricted foreign corporations that can manufacture and sell their goods for less.

Today, all countries are threatened by pollution created in other nations. Many environmentalists argue that a nation's security assessment must take into account threats from environmental causes as well as military and economic threats. They claim that pollution, global warming, deforestation, and ozone depletion could threaten world peace and stability even more than military conflicts.

No nation can close its borders to its neighbors' pollution. For example, air pollution in Mexican border towns affects the air quality in southern Texas and Arizona. Fires in Brazil's tropical forests cause the release of carbon dioxide into the atmosphere, which some scientists believe may change climate patterns. Environmentalists also cite other potential problems including international disputes over shrinking natural resources such as water, forests, and fisheries. They fear that developing countries could go to war over drinking water, food, or fuel.

Over the last fifteen years, environmental problems have become an important aspect of international relations. Many countries have negotiated agreements

Industrial development has spread pollution around the globe. The world's air contains many pollutants, some of which may change global climate patterns, harm human health, and destroy the protective ozone layer in the atmosphere.

According to the Worldwatch Institute, an inventory of wind resources in the United States by the Department of Energy indicates that three states—North Dakota, South Dakota, and Texas—have enough harnessable wind energy to fill electricity needs nationwide.

to reduce pollution worldwide and have joined together to find solutions to the most pressing environmental problems including acid rain, global warming, deforestation, and ozone depletion.

ACID RAIN

Although the causes of acid rain are in dispute, most scientists believe that it is the result of sulfur dioxide and nitrogen oxide (released by coal-burning power plants, factories, and automobiles) being transformed into sulfate and nitrate. When combined with moisture in the air, sulfates and nitrates become acids and fall to the earth as acid rain. Such rain increases the acidity of soil, streams, and lakes, making them less healthy environments for plants and animals. It also corrodes metal, discolors paint, and deteriorates stone.

The effects of acid rain can be seen worldwide. In Europe, where coal has long been a major source of energy, large forests are withering, and hundreds of lakes in Scandinavia are so acidic that they can no longer support fish. Great Britain and Sweden are also affected by acid rain pollution originating in eastern Europe. Acid rain created in the United States crosses the border into Canada.

One way nations can reduce acid rain is by lowering sulfur emissions. For example, U.S. environmental laws required coal-burning plants to reduce their annual sulfur dioxide emissions from 18.9 million tons in 1980 to 8.9 million tons by 2000. Many plants have installed expensive antipollution equipment—called scrubbers— or have switched to using low-sulfur coal.

THE GREENHOUSE EFFECT

During the last 100 years, the level of carbon dioxide in Earth's atmosphere has risen sharply. Some scientists assert that carbon dioxide emissions cause a *greenhouse effect* because they trap the sun's heat, thereby raising the temperature of the atmosphere. Global warming could lead to serious environmental problems, although scientific evidence indicating a greenhouse effect has been inconclusive.

In January 2000, the National Academy of Science's National Research Council released a study showing that Earth's surface temperatures had increased over the past century at between 0.7 and 1.4 degrees Fahrenheit. Estimates for warming in the next century vary from between 2 and 7 degrees Fahrenheit. Some scientists predict that temperatures just a few degrees higher than normal would melt polar ice caps, flood coastal areas, and alter weather patterns around the world. Ice caps and glaciers around the world are already melting.

According to the Worldwatch Institute, a team of U.S. and British scientists reported in mid-1999 that the two ice shelves on either side of the Antarctic peninsula are melting at an accelerated rate. In the fifty years before 1997, the ice shelves lost a total of 7,000 square kilometers, but from 1997 to early 1999, 3,000 square kilometers of ice melted.

Carbon dioxide enters the atmosphere from the burning of fossil fuels such as coal, natural gas, and oil, which supply about 85 percent of energy needs worldwide. Automobiles, factories, and power plants in industrialized countries contribute to Earth's carbon dioxide buildup. It is also released when trees decay or burn. Some developing nations are cutting down or burning their tropical forests for farmland, releasing harmful levels of carbon dioxide into the atmosphere.

Global warming was at the top of the agenda at the 1992 United Nations Conference on Environment and Development—the "Earth Summit"—in Rio de Janeiro, Brazil. At the Earth Summit, world leaders attempted to create a new global treaty to reduce greenhouse gases. However, disagreements emerged. Industrial and non-industrial countries have differing views on how to reduce greenhouse gas emissions and who should pay for those efforts. In addition, scientists remain divided over the issue of global warming—whether it is, in fact, a true long-term trend—as well as its causes and consequences. Thus, nations have found it difficult to agree on the enforcement of emissions reductions goals, and targets set at the Earth Summit have rarely been met.

In December 1997, more than 160 nations met in Kyoto, Japan, to negotiate a legally binding, internationally enforceable protocol. The Kyoto Protocol states specific emissions reduction goals for individual nations. Under the treaty, thirty-eight industrialized countries, including the United States, would be required to lower emissions of six greenhouse gases by 2012. On average, nations would reduce emission levels by 5 percent. The Kyoto Protocol will not take effect until it has been ratified by fifty-five nations that contribute at least 55 percent of the world's carbon dioxide emissions. Representatives from 173 nations met in Bonn, Germany, in November 1999 at a second Climate Change Conference to pressure industrialized countries—including the United States—to ratify the Kyoto Protocol. However, U.S. officials say the United States will not ratify the treaty until developing countries take more action to reduce carbon dioxide emissions.

Human impact on the environment can increase the damage from natural disasters. In 1999, heavy rains caused mudslides along the densely populated Venezuelan coast, killing thousands of people and destroying homes and businesses.

DEFORESTATION

Each year, about 34.6 million acres of tropical forests disappear. Much of the forest is lost to farmers who clear the land to make room for crops and livestock.

Deforestation worries environmentalists for two reasons. First, burning trees contribute to the release of carbon dioxide, which may cause global warming. Since tropical forests can absorb carbon dioxide, their destruction means that more carbon dioxide drifts into the atmosphere. In addition, burning or decaying trees release carbon dioxide into the air. The second reason deforestation worries environmentalists is that when tropical rain forests are destroyed, the animals and plants that live there risk extinction. Scientists estimate that four species—mostly from the tropics—are lost every hour due to deforestation.

At the 1992 UN Earth Summit, world leaders adopted a "Statement on Forest Principles," which states an overall goal of preserving the world's shrinking forests. Some Western conservationist groups are cooperating with foreign governments to prevent farmers from cutting down trees. These groups build dams for irrigation, provide farmers with better seeds, and plant new trees. By improving farming practices near rain forests, they hope that farmers can increase their yields without clearing more trees.

OZONE DEPLETION

Ozone is a gas that is distributed in a thin layer of Earth's atmosphere. Ozone shields Earth from the Sun's ultraviolet rays. These rays can weaken the human immune system, cause skin cancer and eye damage, and destroy crops. Scientists have discovered that some chemicals make the ozone layer thinner, even causing holes, which allow more ultraviolet radiation to reach Earth. In 1985, scientists found a hole in the ozone layer over Antarctica.

Scientists believe that chlorofluorocarbons (CFCs) are a major cause of ozone depletion. CFCs are a family of chemicals that are often used in cleaning solvents and aerosol spray cans and as coolants in refrigerators and air conditioners. CFCs can exist in the atmosphere for as long as 100 years.

In 1987, the industrialized nations signed the Montreal Protocol, which committed them to cutting the use of CFCs in half by 2000. In 1990, a second agreement among sixty-one countries was signed. The new agreement called for a total ban on CFCs by the industrialized countries beginning in 2000. The deadline for developing countries is 2010. Since implementation of these agreements, the number of CFCs in the atmosphere has started to decrease, but scientists say that a strong improvement in the ozone layer will probably not be seen until well into the twenty-first century. In September 2000, NASA measurements showed that the ozone hole had grown to a record 11.4 million square miles and for two days had extended over a populated city—Punta Arenas, Chile—for the first time.

Many scientists believe that global warming, deforestation, and ozone depletion threaten all nations. However, efforts to create global treaties have revealed that nearly every nation brings a different set of environmental circumstances and interests to the negotiating table, which makes building consensus and establishing concrete goals difficult. Although some environmentalists predict that developing nations may some day go to war over scarce resources, others believe that continuing efforts to create global consensus on environmental issues will eventually produce effective environmental treaties and policies.

4.6 THE TWENTY-FIRST CENTURY

Although the international community may be able to cooperate in confronting these issues and problems, nations still fundamentally act in their own self-interest. Global interest has not yet replaced national interest in determining which policies nations pursue.

When world leaders acted to try to stop mass starvation in Somalia and the refugee crisis in Rwanda, they were motivated mostly by a global interest—the alleviation of human suffering. However, most experts agree that, when governments work together to contain nuclear proliferation or expand trade, they are doing so because it is in their own country's self-interest. World leaders generally do not sign free-trade pacts to improve the world's economy so much as to improve their own countries' economies. When European leaders debated how to stop the conflict in Kosovo, they were just as concerned with stopping the problem from getting closer to their own borders as they were about stopping ethnic cleansing. Finding long-term solutions to the economic despair of less-developed countries may be in the global interest, but most industrialized countries do not perceive poorer regions of the world to be strategically or economically important to them. Consequently, their leaders often do not devote much time or money to finding solutions.

However, as long as global interest and national interest continue to overlap on certain issues—international trade, nuclear nonproliferation, containing nationalism, and cleaning up the environment—countries will find themselves working together instead of working separately. Ideally, interdependence, shared interests, and common ideologies will unite, not divide, nations. As a result, international relations in the twenty-first century might be characterized more by cooperation than by conflict, leading the way to a more stable and prosperous world.

APPENDICES

FOR FURTHER READING

The following books and articles will provide information for further research on some of the topics covered in *International Relations*.

THE BEHAVIOR OF NATIONS

"Encounter in Pyongyang." *The Economist*. (17 June 2000): 17, 41–42.

Evans, Graham and Jeffrey Newnham. *Penguin Dictionary of International Relations*. London, England: Penguin Books, 1998.

Friedman, Thomas L. *The Lexus and the Olive Tree: Understanding Globalization*. New York: Anchor Books, 2000.

Haas, Richard N. and Meghan L. O'Sullivan, eds. *Honey and Vinegar: Incentives, Sanctions, and Foreign Policy*. Washington, D.C.: Brookings Institution Press, 2000.

Smith, Dan. *The State of the World Atlas*. Brighton, England: the Penguin Group/Myriad Editions Limited, 1999.

HOW U.S. FOREIGN POLICY IS MADE

Buhite, Russell D., ed. *Major Crises in Contemporary American Foreign Policy: A Documentary History*. Westport, CT: Greenwood Press, 1997.

The Close Up Foundation. *Current Issues 2001: Critical Policy Choices Facing the Nation and the World*. Alexandria, VA: Close Up Foundation, 2000.

Lindsay, James M. "The New Apathy: How an Uninterested Public Is Reshaping Foreign Policy." *Foreign Affairs* 79, no. 5 (2000): 2–8.

Rodman, Peter. "The World's Resentment." *The National Interest* 60 (summer 2000): 33–41.

Thomas J. Watson Jr. Institute for International Studies. *Keeping the Peace in an Age of Conflict: Debating the U.S. Role*. Providence, Rhode Island: Watson Institute for International Studies, Brown University, 1999.

THE COLD WAR AND BEYOND

Alexander, Cynthia J. and Leslie A. Pal, eds. *Digital Democracy: Policy and Politics in the Wired World*. New York: Oxford University Press, 1998.

Chabot, Christian N. *Understanding the Euro*. New York: McGraw–Hill, 1999.

The Close Up Foundation. *Building a Democratic Nation: Governments in Transition.* Alexandria, VA: Close Up Foundation, 2001.

Goldman, Minton F., Dr. *Russia, the Eurasian Republics, and Central/Eastern Europe*, 8th ed. Guilford, Connecticut: Dushkin/McGraw–Hill, 2001.

Segal, Gerald. "Does China Matter?" *Foreign Affairs* 78, no. 5 (1999): 24–36.

WORLD ISSUES TODAY

International Trade

Krugman, Paul. "Has Asia Recovered?" *Time* 154, no. 1(5 July 1999): 48–49.

Paarlberg, Robert. "The Global Food Fight." *Foreign Affairs* 79, no. 3 (2000): 24–38.

Thomas J. Watson Jr. Institute for International Studies. *U.S. Trade Policy: Competing in a Global Economy*, 7th ed. Providence, Rhode Island: Watson Institute for International Studies, Brown University, 2000.

"World Trade." *Congressional Quarterly Researcher* 8, no. 22 (2000): entire issue.

"The World's View of Multinationals." *The Economist* (29 January 2000): 21–22.

Military Buildups

Falkenrath, Richard. "Weapons of Mass Reaction: Rogue States and Weapons of Mass Destruction." *Harvard International Revue* 22, no. 2 (summer 2000): 52–55.

"Missile Defense." *Congressional Quarterly Researcher* 10, no. 30 (2000): entire issue.

Paul, T.V., ed. *The Absolute Weapon Revisited: Nuclear Arms and the Emerging International World Order.* University of Michigan Press, 1998.

Tanter, Raymond. *Rogue Regimes: Terrorism and Proliferation.* New York: St. Martin's Press, 1998.

"Temperatures Rising: India and Pakistan's Explosive Conflict." *World Press* 47, no. 7 (July 2000): 6–11.

Nationalism and Ethnic Conflict

"The Balkans." *Current History* (March 2000): entire issue.

Cozic, Charles P., ed. *Current Controversies: Nationalism and Ethnic Conflict.* San Diego, CA: Greenhaven Press, 1995.

Enriquez, Juan. "Too Many Flags?" *Foreign Policy* 116 1999): 30–49.

Fuller, Graham E. and Rajan Menon. "Russia's Ruinous Chechen War." *Foreign Affairs* 79, no. 2 (2000): 32–44.

Gourevitch, Phillip. *We Wish to Inform You That Tomorrow We Will Be Killed with Our Families: Stories from Rwanda.* Farrar, Straus & Giroux, 1998.

The Developing World

"The Dictatorship of Debt." *World Press Review* 46, no. 10 (October 1999): 6–13.

Egendorf, Laura K., ed. *Opposing Viewpoints: The Third World.* San Diego, CA: Greenhaven Press, 2000.

Eldredge, N. "Will Malthus Be Right?" *Time* 154, no. 19 (1999): 102–103.

Gellman, Barton. "Death Watch: The Belated Global Response to AIDS in Africa." *The Washington Post.* (5 July, 2000) A1.

The World Bank. *Assessing Aid: What Works, What Doesn't, and Why.* Oxford University Press, 1998.

The Environment

"Energy and the Environment." *Congressional Quarterly Researcher* 10, no. 8 (2000): entire issue.

"Welcome to the Greenhouse Century." *The Environmental Magazine* 11, no. 5 (September/October 2000): entire issue.

Nash, J. Madeleine. "Grains of Hope." *Time* 156, no. 5 (31 July 2000): 39–46.

Sarewitz, Daniel and Roger Pielke Jr. "Breaking the Global Warming Gridlock." *Atlantic Monthly* 286, no. 1 (July 2000): 54–64.

Starke, Linda, ed. *State of the World 2000: A Worldwatch Institute Report on Progress Toward a Sustainable Society.* New York: W.W. Norton & Company, Inc., 2000.

WEB RESOURCES

The following Web sites should help you learn more about the topics covered in this book.

CIA World Factbook
www.odci.gov/cia/publications/factbook

Council on Foreign Relations, Inc.
www.foreignaffairs.org/links.html

Freedom House
www.freedomhouse.org

Policy.com
www.policy.com/hotspots

United Nations
www.un.org

U.S. Department of Energy
www.energy.gov

U.S. Department of State
www.state.gov

University of Michigan Documents Center
www.lib.umich.edu/libhome/Documents.center/forpol.html

The World Bank Group
www.worldbank.org

GLOSSARY

alliance—an association of nations that agree to protect each other in case of attack by an adversary

ambassador—a nation's highest-ranking diplomat who resides in an assigned foreign country, represents his or her nation's interest, and reports home on major developments in the host country

bilateral aid—foreign aid that is granted by one nation directly to another nation

bipolarity—the division of global power between two nations

boycott—a decision by one nation or group to abstain from buying certain goods or to refuse to participate in international events to try to force a particular government to change its policies

concert of power—a coalition of powerful nations that work together to maintain the balance of power and promote global economic prosperity

containment—a U.S. Cold War strategy to stop the spread of communism

developing country—a nation with a relatively low level of industrial production and low standard of living

diplomatic immunity—international law that protects diplomats and their families from being arrested or tried for a crime in their host country

diplomatic relations—formal contacts between national governments

diversified economy—an economy that is not dependent on a single crop or industry

domino theory—a Cold War theory which held that if one country became communist, its neighbors would soon "fall" as well

European Union—an economic and security arrangement comprised of fifteen western European nations

floating exchange system—a monetary system in which the value of currencies relative to one another is free to change daily

foreign aid—cash, equipment, or technical advice given by wealthy nations to other countries to gain and protect allies, promote development, and foster internal stability; foreign aid can come in the form of economic or military aid

foreign policy—a course of action developed by a country's leaders to pursue the national interests of that nation

geopolitics—the influence of geography and population on foreign policy

globalization—the trend toward more open and free worldwide trade and interaction

greenhouse effect—environmental problem that occurs when carbon dioxide emissions trap the sun's heat, raising the temperature of the atmosphere

industrialized nation—country with a relatively high standard of living and high level of economic productivity

international relations—how countries relate to one another, how they work together, and how they conflict

limited military response—short-term military action designed to force another nation to back down in a specific dispute and possibly to resolve the conflict through diplomacy

malnutrition—a lack of proper vitamins and nutrients in one's diet

multilateral aid—foreign aid granted through an international organization to which many nations contribute

multipolar—distribution of global power among a number of nations

nation—a centralized political system, with recognized borders and a territory, that governs the population therein

national interest—what is deemed best for a nation's security, economic, and ideological concerns

nationalism—sentiment that people have when they see themselves as a distinct group on the basis of common ancestry, history, society, institutions, ideology, language, territory, and sometimes religion

national resolve—a people's shared beliefs about national interests and strong desire to achieve them

natural resources—materials and capacities (such as coal, oil, timber, waterpower, and minerals) provided by nature

North-South gap—economic difference between nations in the Northern and Southern Hemispheres; created by the North's increasing wealth and the South's continuous poverty

nuclear deterrence—a defense strategy in which a nation's nuclear strength discourages an enemy from initiating nuclear attack, for fear of massive retaliation

propaganda—one-sided or exaggerated information used by a nation to gain both national and international support for its policies or to discredit the policies of an adversary

protectionism—the use of trade restrictions to protect a domestic market from foreign imports or to discriminate against products exported by another nation

quotas—limits on the amount of goods that can be imported

regionalization—division of the world into regional blocs of power and trade

sanction—an action taken by one or more nations to force another nation to comply with international law or to change its policies

self-determination—the right of all people to choose their own form of government

separatism—a form of nationalism in which a group within an already-recognized state wants to form its own country

sphere of influence—area of the world that was loyal to either the United States or to the Soviet Union during the Cold War

summit—a meeting between heads of state

superpower—a nation that has an extremely powerful and dominant economy and military

tariff—a tax on imports

terrorism—acts of violence or destruction carried out by nongovernmental groups that want to gain attention for their political causes

treaty—a formal written agreement between two nations (bilateral treaty) or among three or more nations (multilateral treaty)

undernourishment—a lack of protein and calories in one's diet

ALSO FROM CLOSE UP PUBLISHING

Building a Democratic Nation:
Governments in Transition

Current Issues:
Critical Policy Choices Facing the Nation and the World

The Breakup of the Soviet Union:
U.S.-Russian Relations Ten Years Later

The United Nations at Work:
The Challenge of Building Global Peace

U.S. Response:
The Making of U.S. Foreign Policy (simulation)

Ordinary Americans: The Red Scare (video)

Close Up Publishing
44 Canal Center Plaza
Alexandria, VA 22314-1592
800-765-3131
www.closeup.org/pubs.htm